Of Men and Materiel

Of Men and Materiel

The Crisis in Military Resources

Edited by
Gary J. Schmitt and Thomas Donnelly

The AEI Press

Publisher for the American Enterprise Institute
WASHINGTON, D.C.

Distributed to the Trade by National Book Network, 15200 NBN Way, Blue Ridge Summit, PA 17214. To order call toll free 1-800-462-6420 or 1-717-794-3800. For all other inquiries please contact the AEI Press, 1150 Seventeenth Street, N.W., Washington, D.C. 20036 or call 1-800-862-5801.

Library of Congress Cataloging-in-Publication Data

   Of men and materiel : the crisis in military resources / edited by Gary
J. Schmitt and Thomas Donnelly.
      p. cm.

   ISBN-13: 978-0-8447-4249-6 (pbk : alk. paper)
   ISBN-10: 0-8447-4249-X

   1. United States—Armed Forces—Operational readiness. 2. United
States—Armed Forces—Procurement. 3. United States—Armed
Forces—Recruiting, enlistment, etc. 4. United States—Military
policy. I. Schmitt, Gary James, 1952- II. Donnelly, Thomas, 1953-
I. Title.

   UA23.O36 2007
   355.20973—dc22

                                                        2006100737

   12 11 10 09 08 07   1 2 3 4 5 6

Printed in the United States of America

Contents

Introduction

The following chapters were written to examine each of the military services and the Marine Corps with an eye toward what resources they will need in order to meet America's strategic needs, rather than what current and projected budgets will allow.

In the first chapter, "Numbers Matter," we attempt to place the current crisis in defense resources in a broader strategic and historical context. The fact that there is a crisis at all will certainly come as a surprise to many. Most Americans assume that the growth in defense spending since September 11, 2001, has corrected the widely reported gap between military means and ends that developed during the 1990s. But, as we point out, much of this increase has gone toward fighting wars in Afghanistan and Iraq and paying for the rising personnel costs associated with America's all-volunteer force. Far less has gone toward replenishing the military's equipment and platforms or increasing the size of the Army and the Marine Corps. The result has been a "hollow buildup" that makes it increasingly difficult for the American military to carry out confidently its role in support of the national security strategy.

In chapter 2, "Protracted Wars and the Army's Future," Frederick Kagan outlines the ways in which the U.S. military has come to rely too heavily on technology and to underappreciate the importance of large and ready ground forces. Fifteen years of wars and peacekeeping operations show that long-term postconflict deployments are the norm rather than the exception. And, indeed, for a lack of "boots on the ground" today, the American military's ability to wage successfully the wars in Iraq and Afghanistan has been substantially hampered. To meet the nation's current needs and be prepared to respond to possible future military crises, Kagan argues, America's ground forces must be dramatically expanded.

According to Loren Thompson in chapter 3, "Age and Indifference Erode U.S. Air Power," the failure to fund an adequate modernization program for the Air Force has jeopardized perhaps the single most important warfighting advantage the United States currently enjoys. Living off previous military buildups, America's air fleet has aged significantly and is showing signs of decline—including a decline in the Air Force's relative superiority against potential adversaries. The future of U.S. air power, Thompson writes, depends on acquiring a sufficient number of next-generation airframes, most notably the F-22 fighter, the C-17 transport, the KC-X tanker, and a future long-range bomber. Compounding these problems is a muddled space program whose costs have skyrocketed but whose actual programs are languishing.

Robert Work makes the case in chapter 4, "Numbers and Capabilities: Building a Navy for the Twenty-First Century," that, despite its relatively small size in comparison with past U.S. fleets, today's Navy operates the most powerful battle fleet the United States has ever put to sea, and is by far the most capable naval force in the world. However, the Navy's current plan to sustain maritime dominance, as embodied in its planned fleet of 313 ships, is problematic, resting as it does on a series of overly optimistic assumptions about the costs of acquiring new ships and holding down costs in other naval programs. The danger, Work argues, is that the Navy in the years ahead will find itself caught in a shipbuilding program that it cannot execute and, equally important, poorly positioned to surge new naval capabilities to meet threats that are only now appearing on the horizon. To maintain naval supremacy now and in the future, he offers an alternative, less expensive plan for expanding the fleet.

In the volume's final chapter, "The Marine Corps: A Hybrid Force for a Hybrid World," Francis Hoffman points out that, traditionally, the Marine Corps has been configured partly for amphibious warfare and partly to handle military "brush fires" and "small wars." Recently, however, because of the pressing nature of the conflicts in Iraq and Afghanistan and constraints on the Corps' budget, experts inside and outside the Pentagon have suggested that the Marines should shed their naval legacy and devote themselves to the global war on terror. Hoffman argues that such a change would be shortsighted and details the geopolitical reasons why the Corps should retain an amphibious capability, while still meeting the challenges posed by irregular warfare. It is a hybrid capacity that the Marines are uniquely qualified to maintain and one the nation will be hard-pressed to do without.

Each of our authors was chosen because of his recognized expertise with respect to a particular branch of the military. There was no effort to fine-edit their contributions to have them fit a predetermined formula. Although we believe that more money needs to be spent on the military to close the gap between America's global military requirements and its military means, the point of the chapters, as will be clear to readers, is not simply to throw money at the problem. But, as the saying goes, one can't get something for nothing—and that is undoubtedly true in the case of military hardware and the men and women who will be employing it.

Nor are we arguing that more cannot be done to bring into being a more rational procurement system—one that develops and fields new weapons in a more timely and cost-effective way. But that is a study and a book for another day. Moreover, waiting for that long-standing problem to be solved before taking on the task of recapitalizing the American military is akin to asking the government to end all waste, fraud, and abuse before we let it govern. In the meantime, America's military will suffer for lack of needed resources. The fact is, when the country moved from a conscript force to an all-volunteer force, it undertook an implicit contract with those who joined the military: In exchange for their willingness to put their lives on the line as a career, the country pledged that their pay, benefits, and deployments would allow them to raise their families in a somewhat normal way, and that the training and equipment provided them would be superior to those of any adversary they might be asked to face in combat. This is a contract we need to keep.

Nevertheless, there is within military reformist circles today a view that "necessity is the mother of invention," and that increasing the military budget will only feed a bureaucratic beast that knows no limit. And, certainly, no one who is familiar with the ways of the Pentagon thinks that every decision made by the services and the Corps on what they need to do their jobs will be optimal or even right. But, that said, at the end of the day a military that has less will do less.

So, by all means, Congress, the Pentagon, industry, and experts should all work on fixing the procurement mess and continue to ask America's military leaders hard questions about why they want this or that particular system or to continue to operate in ways that may no longer make sense. But, as a country, we should also recognize that an underfunded and undermanned military is a far more urgent issue than the failure to turn the Pentagon into a model of hyperefficiency and paradigm-breaking military thinking. The latter is a problem; the former is a recipe for defeat.

1

Numbers Matter

Gary J. Schmitt and Thomas Donnelly

At the end of the nineteenth century, American politicians and policymakers began to grasp that the geopolitical position of the United States was changing profoundly. Not only had the country's economy become the largest in the world, but its ability to stand aloof from international politics had disappeared: the rise of Germany made the European balance of power increasingly unstable, and that of Japan posed a potential challenge to existing and growing American interests in East Asia.

"We cannot," wrote Theodore Roosevelt at the time, "sit huddled within our own borders and avow ourselves merely an assemblage of well-to-do hucksters who care nothing for what happens beyond. Such a policy would defeat even its own end." As nations came into increasingly close economic and political contact, he argued, the United States would have to acquire the means that would "enable us to have our say in deciding the destiny of the oceans of the East and West."[1]

The essential task Roosevelt and likeminded men set for themselves, then, was to match American means with American ends. And while they defined the realm of "means" broadly, it was clear that an essential measure of the nation's rising power would be its capability to protect its increasingly global interests. To attain such capability, Roosevelt argued for a military, especially a navy, sized and structured not only for immediate defense of the American homeland, but also able to project power both in its own hemisphere and in the distant quarters of the world.

As war with Spain over Cuba loomed, Roosevelt and others worried that the U.S. military was not adequately prepared. In the 1880s Congress had begun a modest naval rearmament effort, but it was premised upon the traditional policy of commerce-raiding, the *guerre de course*, and the supposition that the British Royal Navy would handle any serious fighting. In the event, the U.S. Navy proved itself more than a match for Spain's navy, but the Spanish fleet was no more than second-rate by the standards of the great powers. And who knew whether Britain would always and everywhere be sympathetic to U.S. interests? The difficulties of projecting power simultaneously in both their own hemisphere (Cuba) and in Asia (the Philippines) convinced a large segment of the American public that U.S. military forces were in need of an upgrade in both quality and quantity. When Roosevelt became president in 1901, he was able to push through not one but two significant shipbuilding projects.

Roosevelt understood the gap between America's growing strategic vision and its lagging military means. When, for example, tensions rose with Japan during his second term, he found that any notion of sending the fleet to the Pacific was a nonstarter. "Splitting the fleet" was a cardinal sin to tacticians of the time. Moreover, the fleet was not really large enough to split. The president thought briefly of sending four battleships to the Pacific but decided that the risk was not worth the reward.

This dilemma defined what would be the fundamental problem for the U.S. Navy through the 1930s: How much fleet was enough to operate effectively in both the Atlantic and Pacific theaters, able to fight on two fronts simultaneously? Even as the questions of capability were resolved—Roosevelt again played the leading role in 1905 by deciding in favor of all big-gun ships of the line—the size of the force remained at issue. The benchmark was a two-ocean fleet, but it was not until Franklin Roosevelt confronted the requirements of a two-front war against Imperial Japan and Nazi Germany that the question was decided in favor of the "Big Navy Boys," who argued for a fleet that was "second to none."[2]

Numbers have always mattered in American military history, but especially so since the United States has become a world power.

Force size and geopolitical goals—means and ends—are the intertwined double helix that carries the codes for successful strategy-making. When the two strands are in healthy balance, the United States has been able to defend itself and its interests and to advance its principles.

Today, however, we hear from senior Pentagon officials that, in fact, "It's not about numbers. Numbers don't tell you if you can get the job done."[3] And, of course, at one level that is true. Scores of wooden U.S. cruisers would have been no match for Chile's iron-clad ships of the line in the 1880s or 1890s. And, more recently, a large Iraqi army was no match for the high-tech, highly mobile military that the United States used to bring down Saddam Hussein's regime. But, that said, men, planes, and ships cannot be in two places at once, no matter how capable. One only has to see how "stretched thin" America's land forces are today with the ongoing operations in both Iraq and Afghanistan to worry that another major crisis will leave us in a very difficult situation. Quantity has a qualitative aspect of its own that we ignore at our peril if we wish to ensure that our military means match our global interests and obligations. Numbers do, in fact, matter.

"More Difficult Than Expected"

Teddy Roosevelt's problem was matching America's military means to the country's global interests and new role in the world. That problem remains.

For many years, the problem was defined by a discussion of what it would take to deter the Soviet Union and its allies or, in the worst case, defeat them in battle. Although never an easy strategic problem to solve, it was somewhat predictable and, without a direct military confrontation having occurred between the two superpowers, the various military strategies for dealing with it were, thankfully, never put to the test. However, with the collapse of the Soviet Union, the United States was left standing as the globe's "sole superpower," presiding over what seemed to be a largely stable and peaceful world, yet of a very mixed mind on what would come next.

George Herbert Walker Bush was the first president to confront this question. He was schooled in the tactics of the Cold War, a struggle in which the enemy was thought to be understood and whose military provided an omnipresent measuring stick for U.S. forces. With the collapse of the Warsaw Pact, Bush faced a fundamental, first-order question about strategy. The how-much-is-enough debate of the previous fifty years became how much is enough—and for what?

This question caught Bush and his lieutenants off-guard. The "unipolar moment" was not something they or, for that matter, anybody else had thought much about. Nevertheless, it was the reality they were forced to deal with. An argument was advanced, mostly by strategists in the Department of Defense, that taking advantage of American primacy would achieve a lasting change in international politics and accelerate the global trend toward democratic forms of government. But to men steeped in the strategic calculus of the Cold War, the opportunity of this new moment was displaced by arguments about the reduced level of threat the country faced. And so, when it came to military planning, the Bush administration moved cautiously toward the so-called Base Force, a force structure that was to represent a modest downsizing of the military of the late 1980s. It would be a very capable force due to the new weaponry purchased in the Reagan years, but smaller in terms of active-duty personnel than the Reagan-era total of 2.1 million.

Since the end of the Cold War and the ongoing implosion of the Soviet Union had removed almost any sense of an external threat, the purpose of the Base Force plan, claimed General Colin Powell, then chairman of the Joint Chiefs of Staff, was to set out a sign proclaiming, "Superpower lives here."[4] Its primary purpose was to deter new threats from appearing, not to respond to any clear or present danger. Numbers still mattered, but determining how much force would be enough became something of an arbitrary exercise. The Bush administration envisioned a military about 15 percent smaller than the force of the late 1980s—enough, it was thought, to guard against Russian revanchism, deter regional powers with possible hegemonic ambitions, and respond to unforeseen but passing contingencies. The primary concern was the immediate task of ushering the Soviet Union to its grave, with less thought given to the nature of the post-Soviet international order; the administration—and, for that matter, the country—acted as though it were living through "the end of history."[5] As a result, political pressure to maintain federal fiscal discipline and cut the defense budget was growing stronger than any abstract strategic rationales for maintaining a large military establishment in the absence of an obvious threat.

Nevertheless, because the leadership within the Bush administration's Pentagon was fundamentally conservative in its approach to defense planning, what it was able to maintain in the short term turned out to be militarily sound. Less than six weeks after the fall of the Berlin Wall, in December 1989, an airborne *coup de main* removed the noxious regime of Panamanian strongman Manuel Noriega. Operation Just Cause was touted as a model of modern military art: rapid, decisive, and relatively low in casualties (only twenty-six Americans died and a little over two hundred Panamanians were killed). The Pentagon and the administration downplayed the fact that U.S. forces had been in Panama for decades, that much of the fighting took place within sight of the U.S. Southern Command headquarters, and that the fall of the Noriega regime was followed by a collapse of public order and looting. Just Cause was taken as a paradigm for post–Cold War operations: quick and clean, maximizing the professionalism and technological advantages of U.S. forces. The surprising success of the operation confirmed to the administration that its strategic views were correct, and that its long-term defense plan could proceed.

Within nine months, however, Iraqi dictator Saddam Hussein had put a hitch in the step of those who thought the post–Cold War era would be one dominated by diplomacy, economics, and soft power. Sensing that the August 1990 invasion of Kuwait was a direct challenge to American interests and the emerging post–Cold War international order, President Bush orchestrated both a diplomatic and military response to restore the Kuwaiti emirate and the status quo and to prevent any regional hegemon from dominating the oil-rich Persian Gulf region.

As a military matter, Saddam could hardly have chosen a worse moment to confront the United States. U.S. forces had received much of the benefit of the Reagan buildup but had yet to undergo much in the way of the planned reductions; the force was both relatively large and extremely capable. Once Saudi Arabia consented to host American troops, at first in defense of the kingdom but then as a staging base for a counteroffensive into Kuwait, General Powell assured that the outcome would never be in doubt. From September 1990 to the following January, U.S. forces streamed into the theater to defend Saudi Arabia, with an armada that included six aircraft carriers, thousands of aircraft, and about a quarter million ground troops. When the air war began on January 17, 1991, heavy land forces continued to flow into Saudi Arabia. After thirty-eight days of intense bombardment, theater commander Army General H. Norman Schwarzkopf unleashed a huge ground force of over a half million, with British, French, Gulf Arab, and coalition forces augmenting U.S. soldiers and Marines. The victory was so certain that, at the last moment, Syria wanted to get in on the attack and sent an armored division.

In the course of recovering Kuwait, the Bush administration also hoped to destroy a substantial portion of Iraq's offensive military capability; removing Saddam from power wasn't necessary, but reducing his ability to destabilize the Gulf was. Although a few mechanized units escaped north of the Euphrates River, about 50 percent of the Republican Guard in the area was destroyed in just one hundred hours of fighting by the massive and maneuvering American, British, and French armored forces. The Bush administration could fairly say it had met its objective: Iraq no longer possessed the capability to upset the broader regional balance of power.

The victory seemed complete, and an even more stunning display of American military supremacy than the Panama operation. American casualties were again small. Particularly impressive were the clear advances in precision-strike airpower. Airpower had become, it seemed, the very essence of American military power, conferring a psychological aspect that magnified its invincibility;

U.S. air forces could strike at will anywhere they chose, and the enemy could not prevent it.[6]

But the very success of Operation Desert Storm convinced many strategists and politicians that defense cutbacks were justified because American military power was so overwhelming. It was seen as excessive, and, in what was emerging as a time of great-power peace, unnecessary. War itself seemed almost obsolescent. Any enemy—particularly a petty tyrant of the Saddam Hussein sort— rash or foolish enough to provoke an American military response could look forward to similar treatment: a pounding from the air followed by a mop-up land campaign, the latter of which might not even be required. The Desert Storm model lived on in formal defense planning as a major regional conflict—an MRC—whose details might differ depending on geography, but whose outcome was little in doubt.

And so defense budgets became increasingly driven by domestic politics and the cry for a post–Cold War "peace dividend." With no serious enemies on the horizon, with U.S. forces enjoying such supremacy, and with a sluggish economy, the incoming Clinton administration moved rapidly to slice Bush's Base Force by another 20 percent, with the spending reductions weighted heavily toward cuts in weapons programs. The Navy, for example, was set on a path to reducing its fleet by about 150 ships. Colin Powell called the Clinton plan "fundamentally flawed," leaving U.S. forces "unbalanced."[7]

But even as the Clinton administration's 1993 "bottom-up review" of the defense posture pressed for a deeper drawdown of U.S. forces, it established an expansive vision of what this reduced force would be able to achieve: It was to be ready to respond to two major regional contingencies, nearly simultaneously.[8] With post-Soviet Europe seemingly at peace, Pentagon planners believed that U.S. forces should be able to deploy, fight, and decisively win a war in Southwest Asia (with Iraq the canonical candidate for further chastisement) and in Northeast Asia (North Korea fit the bill as a likely enemy) more or less at once. The position of the United States as the dominant global power demanded that its military be able to patrol an ever-larger perimeter, protecting its allies and interests and responding rapidly to threats. The question was, could this smaller force meet those commitments?

The gap between means and ends led critics, especially in the Republican-controlled Congress, to charge Clinton's administration with being weak on defense. The decline in defense resources not only seemed to invite risk but cut at the core of the defense industrial base built over five decades of Cold War procurement. The program reductions and resultant loss of high-wage manufacturing jobs were keenly felt in key congressional districts. Moreover, the Clinton administration was nearly schizophrenic when it came to the use of military force. It never escaped the fumbling approach that doomed the intervention in Somalia, which was begun at the end of the Bush term but resulted in the "Black Hawk Down" incident in Mogadishu in 1993 and the ignominious withdrawal in early 1994 (a withdrawal that made a lasting impression on a Saudi radical and millionaire named Osama bin Laden). Saddam Hussein remained a raw sore; eventually, twice as many air sorties were flown enforcing the Northern Watch and Southern Watch no-fly-zone operations as during the 1991 Gulf War. And although the administration managed finally to rally a coalition to put an end to Slobodan Milosevic's ethnic cleansing of the former Yugoslavia, the slow-motion genocide was as much evidence of American weakness as of American strength.

Increasingly, Republicans in charge of the House and Senate armed services committees were in no mood to defer to the executive on defense matters. There was a strong feeling on Capitol Hill that Clinton-era defense reductions had gone too far, and in 1996, Congress passed the Military Force Structure Review Act, directing the Pentagon to undertake

> a comprehensive examination of defense strategy, force structure, modernization plans, infrastructure, budget plan, and other elements of the defense program and policies with a view toward determining and expressing the defense strategy of the United States

and establishing a revised [future years] defense program through the year 2005.[9]

The administration's response was to establish the Quadrennial
Defense Review (QDR) process, with the first review to be completed in 1997. Uncertain, however, that the QDR would produce
a review that met the standards of the 1996 law, Congress mandated a separate National Defense Panel (NDP) of independent
experts and former officers. The panel's two tasks were to grade the
administration's work on the 1997 QDR and to produce its own
review of the U.S. defense posture.

The 1997 review was a measure of the Clinton administration's
incoherence. Taking a Polonius-like approach to the exercise, the
Pentagon recommended a plan for shaping the "international security environment in ways that are favorable to U.S. interests" but
continuing to reduce forces stationed abroad. It also promised to
"respond to crises"—an attempt to maintain the two-big-war standard, although the response to the two crises would come "in close
succession" rather than the previous "nearly simultaneously."
Further, crises might also include "small-scale contingencies," like
Panama, Somalia, or, more pressingly, the Balkans wars, which had
at last provoked an American and European response in the form
of a 60,000-man stabilization force deployed in 1996.

Finally, the 1997 QDR looked farther ahead to the day when a
rising great power might again challenge the larger international
order, and new technologies would change the way wars are fought.
The review intended to prepare the Pentagon to exploit a "revolution in military affairs." Looking in three strategic directions, the
Clinton administration offered three different force structures
and investment plans. The first was to continue to postpone equipment modernization, but keep active-duty troop strength at the
current 1.4 million; the second was to emphasize modernization,
increasing procurement accounts to about $65 billion per year
(or about half the Reagan-era peak) while trimming troop levels
to 1.3 million; the third plan split the difference.[10] None of the
plans was premised on any significant increase in overall defense

spending, which, despite the booming economy, had by 1998 fallen to $268.5 billion, or 3.1 percent of the gross domestic product (GDP).

The 1997 defense review pleased few. The Republicans who headed the defense committees in Congress were unhappy about the levels of overall defense spending and the continued need for procurement cuts. Yet these legislators were not even a majority within their own party. The Republicans who had swept into power in 1994 and made domestic issues their priority were leery of all federal government programs and tended to view military procurement as riddled with waste. The Republican leader, House Speaker Newt Gingrich, promised to "turn the Pentagon into a triangle," meaning that its bureaucracy needed serious reform before it could be trusted with new infusions of cash.

Indeed, Gingrich's views were in line with the thinking of the National Defense Panel. The panel's report emphasized a need to exploit the revolution in military affairs, advancing what it called a "strategy of transformation"—an approach that measured success not by victory on the battlefield, externally, but by the pace of internal change. The panel was taken with the idea that the immediate post–Cold War world represented a "strategic pause." During that period, it concluded, "we are unlikely to see an opponent who can successfully counter our military strength directly. . . . We are in a relatively secure interlude following an era of intense international confrontation." In a time of "uncertainty," the one certainty the panel could agree upon was that "the greatest danger lies in an unwillingness or inability to change our security posture in time to meet the challenges of the next century."[11]

The NDP was sharply critical of the two-war standard that had guided the 1997 QDR and its predecessors. "The Panel views the two-military-theater-of-war construct as a force-sizing function and not a strategy," its report sniffed. "We are concerned that this construct may have become . . . a means of justifying the current force structure. . . . It is fast becoming an inhibitor to reaching the capabilities we need [in the future]."[12] The report was not well received by congressional defense barons and drew a sharp rebuff from Defense Secretary William Cohen, the former Republican senator from Maine:

> Given America's enduring global interests and today's serious security challenges on the Korean Peninsula and in Southwest Asia—challenges that are explicitly recognized by the Panel—I believe that maintaining a capability, in concert with allies, to fight and win two major theater wars in overlapping time frames remains central to credibly deterring opportunism and aggression in these critical regions. Moreover, this level of capability helps ensure that the United States maintains sufficient military capabilities over the longer term to deter or defeat aggression by an adversary that proves to be more capable than current foes or under circumstances that prove to be more difficult than expected.[13]

"More difficult than expected" was a phrase that echoed within the Clinton administration as it learned from experience that "assertive multilateralism" was more a hope than a reality; that faced with a recalcitrant Saddam, a war-waging Milosevic, a dangerous North Korea, and a rapidly rising China, military power mattered; and that numbers of forces mattered. In the administration's eyes, America had become the "indispensable nation"; in the eyes of the French, it was a "hyperpuissance"—not simply a superpower, but a hyperpower dictating the terms of international politics.[14]

But with Clinton's days in office waning, the real debate was taking place between the more conservative defense barons in Congress and the advocates of transformation. The leadership in the armed services committees wanted first to rebuild and restore the current forces and was willing to pay for it; the transformationists wanted first to change the nature of U.S. forces. Some enthusiasts, like those on the NDP, went so far as to argue that increasing defense budgets would forestall the revolution. Necessity would be the mother of invention, or so they argued. In any case, the result was a stalemate that continued through the remainder of President Clinton's term in office.

The stalemate, however, had consequences. During the eight Clinton years, the size of the U.S. military was reduced by more than a half million troops, active and reserve. Generally, the United States had one-third fewer Army divisions, battleships, and attack and fighter aircraft.[15] Moreover, hundreds of billions of dollars in planned modernization—both research and procurement funds—were forgone.

And so, by the end of Bill Clinton's second term, the United States had expanded its geopolitical goals yet allowed its military forces to stagnate. The gap between ends and means was growing larger.

"Help Was on the Way"—or Not

Despite America's role in the world over the previous decade having made it demonstrably clear that more military capability was needed, not less, Americans in 2000 believed they still faced no obvious great threat. Predictably, the presidential campaign that year centered on domestic issues. Vice President Al Gore ran on the Clinton legacy of economic growth; he hardly spoke of military affairs. And, on foreign policy, he was content to point out that as vice president he had vastly more experience than his opponent, George W. Bush. But Bush had chosen Dick Cheney, defense secretary during the George H. W. Bush administration and a familiar face during Desert Storm, as his vice presidential running mate. Cheney played on this past and struck at the Clinton administration's military missteps. Candidate Bush also buttressed his qualifications to be commander in chief by surrounding himself with a group of well-known Republican strategic thinkers who became known as "the Vulcans," a term suggesting their clout, experience, and hardheaded views of international politics and power.[16]

Bush also made two powerful campaign speeches that gave him an aura of gravitas on strategy and policy. Fittingly, at the Reagan Library in California, then-governor Bush laid claim to the Reagan legacy, linking the exercise of American power to American political principles, calling for "a distinctly American internationalism," based upon "idealism, without illusions; confidence, without conceit; realism, in the service of American ideals."[17] Bush, in essence, promised to maintain American preeminence but to show better judgment in the use of force than had the Clinton administration. The second speech, given a few weeks earlier at the Citadel, addressed military affairs more directly but invoked the same theme that the post–Cold War world existed in an "era of American preeminence," and asserted that he would work to "turn these years of influence into decades of peace."[18]

Yet, as to means, Bush embraced the vision of the transformationists: "I intend to force new thinking and hard choices," he vowed. In so doing, he sidestepped the question of the size of the defense budget and the military's immediate needs—shortfalls then conservatively estimated by the Joint Chiefs of Staff to be in excess of $150 billion over six years.[19] How, again, the gap between military means and strategic goals was to be resolved went unanswered.

With no record of its own to defend, however, the Republican ticket could and did repeatedly argue that the Clinton administration—and Vice President Al Gore, the Democratic candidate for 2000—had superintended a decade of defense neglect. Vice presidential candidate Dick Cheney promised that "George W. Bush will repair what has been damaged."

> For eight years, Clinton and Gore have extended our military commitments while depleting our military power. Rarely has so much been demanded of our armed forces, and so little given to them in return. George W. Bush and I are going to change that, too. I have seen our military at its finest, with the best equipment, the best training, and the best leadership. I'm proud of them. I have had the responsibility for their well-being. And I can promise them now, help is on the way.[20]

And so it seemed that there would be immediate budget relief for a military—particularly a U.S. Army—struggling with unanticipated global deployments and, especially, with the long-term commitment to the Balkans. To Bush and his Vulcans, however, the most pressing issues—reflecting the "strategic pause" school of thought—were the rise of China as a great power and the need to reinvigorate stalled missile defense efforts. The demands of the constabulary missions in the Balkans and elsewhere were regarded simply as a misuse of U.S. forces. Early on, Bush made it clear that he regarded Beijing as a "strategic competitor," in contradistinction to the Clinton-era "strategic partner." The focus on China also reflected the influence of the transformationists. In considering a potential future crisis or conflict with China, the key operational questions were the vast distances of the East Asia theater and the ability of the People's Liberation Army to develop niche technologies intended to exacerbate the difficulties U.S. forces would face in operating so far from home. The Chinese were thought to be pursuing an anti-access strategy. Solving this problem became a central element in the transformation movement.

The transformationists got another boost when the new President Bush chose Donald Rumsfeld to be his secretary of defense. Upon making the nomination, the president claimed that "effective military power is increasingly defined not by size or mass but by mobility and swiftness." He believed there was

> a great opportunity in America to redefine how wars are fought and won. . . . Our nation is positioned well to use technologies to redefine the military. And one of Secretary Rumsfeld's first tasks will be to challenge the status quo inside the Pentagon, to develop a strategy necessary to have a force equipped for the warfare of the 21st century.[21]

Rumsfeld responded that he had studied carefully the president's Citadel "blueprint," and that he "supported it enthusiastically." He promised to implement radical changes in U.S. military forces.

> You called for America's capabilities to be designed to meet the challenges of the 21st century. It is clearly not

a time at the Pentagon for presiding or calibrating modestly. Rather, we are in a new national security requirement. We need to deal with the new threats, not the old ones . . . with information warfare, missile defense, terrorism, defense of our space assets and the proliferation of weapons of mass destruction throughout the world.[22]

Congressional defense leaders did not immediately grasp the new administration's intentions; a bipartisan delegation—remembering Cheney's "help is on the way" promise—journeyed to Texas prior to the inauguration to push the case for broad-based defense relief and larger budgets. Virginia Republican John Warner, anticipating his return to the chairmanship of the Senate Armed Services Committee, pleaded that defense needs be given "equal billing" in the administration with education and the economy. Democratic Representative John Murtha said he was "impressed" by the president-elect and told Bush, "The people in this room are going to support you on national defense."[23]

Yet the Bush administration chose to submit only a placeholder budget in February 2001, essentially forwarding the request anticipated in the last year of the Clinton era. Not until June did the Bush White House come up with a budget amendment for $18 billion to resolve shortfalls in the Clinton program, with $4.1 billion to cover authorized-but-unfunded pay and benefits costs alone. With the exception of about $600 million in missile defense programs, there was almost nothing new in the 2002 budget. Following the blueprint of the most devoted transformationists, the Bush administration was determined to transform the military within existing budgetary constraints, counting primarily on reduced manpower costs—that is, a smaller force—to offset new research and revived procurement programs. Rumsfeld also made good on Bush's desire to "challenge the status quo within the Pentagon," mainly by means of the 2001 Quadrennial Defense Review. The Army, in particular, was targeted for a reduction from ten active-duty divisions to eight. But as the drawn-out QDR process neared its conclusion, the country was jolted by the terrorist attacks of September 11, 2001. Our "strategic pause" had come to an end.

The Long War

Given the surprise of the terrorist strikes on the World Trade Center and the Pentagon and the foiled attack on Washington, it might seem unfair to view the 2001 QDR as a post-9/11 document. Despite the shock of the moment, however, the Defense Department itself averred that "adapting to surprise—adapting quickly and decisively—must . . . be a condition" of U.S. defense planning.[24] Yet, paradoxically, the 2001 QDR only reinforced and exacerbated the self-referential tendencies of American post–Cold War strategy-making. The central objective of the review "was to shift the basis of defense planning from a 'threat-based' model that has dominated thinking in the past to a 'capabilities-based' model for the future." In other words, rather than take account of a new—or a newly appreciated—threat from al-Qaeda and other radical Islamist organizations, or from the general political instability of the greater Middle East, the Pentagon concluded that the United States simply needed to "maintain its military advantages in key areas while it develops new areas of military advantages and denies asymmetric advantages to adversaries." The 9/11 attacks reinforced the prior belief that transformation itself was the goal, requiring a longstanding commitment from the nation, one that could only "be realized as we divest ourselves of legacy forces . . . [so that] resources move into new concepts, capabilities and organizations."[25] Initially, the Pentagon viewed the military response to 9/11 as a necessary but temporary sidestep on the road to the revolution in military affairs. They certainly did not see it as the opening stage of what would become the long war for the greater Middle East.

The QDR also advanced a new force-sizing construct, replacing the two-major-theater-war benchmark with a more complex 1-4-2-1 structure. The first priority, naturally enough after 9/11, was to defend the American homeland. The second was to maintain a deterrent posture in four regions: Europe, Northeast Asia, maritime East Asia, and the Persian Gulf and Middle East. The review retained as its third priority a watered-down version of the old two-war standard, in the form of a requirement to be able to combat aggression in two theaters simultaneously. And it hoped to minimize the burden and duration of those combat operations by emphasizing rapid deployments, leveraging advances in precision-guided weaponry, and minimizing the deployment of land forces. Thus, the final "one" in the 1-4-2-1 formula was the goal of being able to win decisively in a single major conflict. In effect, the Pentagon was realistically admitting for the first time that it no longer had the force structure required to handle two major wars and was hoping that any other combat operations would be rapidly concluded. It was a risk the Bush administration felt it could take.[26]

The stunning results of the invasions of Afghanistan and Iraq seemed to validate this Pentagon assessment. Overcoming immense logistical challenges, the United States drove the Taliban from power in a matter of months. And after a complex and extended diplomatic dance in the run-up to the invasion of Iraq, major combat operations themselves lasted only from March 18 to April 9, 2003, when Baghdad fell to U.S. forces.

Yet, almost as quickly, it became apparent that the Defense Department had miscalculated the threat: the more difficult and consuming missions would not be the invasions of these distant lands, but their subsequent occupation and reconstruction. Not only did these turn into engagements of long duration, but ones that have placed a premium on manpower over technology and the control of territory over the destruction of enemy forces. In Iraq, particularly, as counterinsurgency has edged closer to internecine sectarian conflict, U.S. forces have found themselves stretched to their limits. These missions highlighted the long-feared asymmetries to which a highly professional yet reduced American military—particularly land forces—was vulnerable. As Lieutenant General David Barno, commander of coalition forces in Afghanistan from 2003 through 2005, has put it, "In Kabul, Americans have all the watches but Afghans have all the time."[27]

The military's surprise at the extent of its postcombat missions underscored a deepening division between the White House's strategic vision and that of the Pentagon. In the period after the invasion of Afghanistan but before Operation Iraqi Freedom, President Bush's view of the nature of post-9/11 strategy had changed profoundly. Here was a man who had sharply criticized the Clinton administration's attempts at nation-building but was announcing a vision and making a commitment to the Middle East that dwarfed his predecessor's efforts in the Balkans and elsewhere. Beginning with the 2002 State of the Union address—best known as the "Axis of Evil" speech—Bush declared that the so-called global war on terror would be a war for democratic revolution, and that "no nation is exempt."[28]

The president continued to define this new and expansive direction for American security strategy, most formally in the 2002 National Security Strategy of the United States, whose "aim . . . is to help make the world not just safer but better."[29] Speaking on September 11, 2002, he made clear the definition and purposes of this "Bush Doctrine":

> There is a line in our time, and in every time, between those who believe men are created equal, and those who believe some men and women and children are expendable in the pursuit of power. There is a line in our time, and in every time, between the defenders of human liberty and those who seek to master the minds and souls of others. Our generation has heard history's call, and we will answer it . . . .
>
> This nation has defeated tyrants and liberated death camps, raised this lamp of liberty to every captive land. We have no intention of ignoring or appeasing history's latest gang of fanatics trying to murder their way into power. They are discovering, as others before them, the resolve of a great country and a great democracy. In the ruins of two towers, under a flag unfurled at the Pentagon, at the funerals of the lost, we have made a

sacred promise to ourselves and the world: we will not relent until justice is done and our nation is secure. What our enemies have begun, we will finish.[30]

The Pentagon seemed not to hear "history's call," nor comprehend the change of mission called for by the commander in chief. Not only did the Afghan and Iraqi campaigns conform to the design for a rapid, decisive operation followed by a speedy withdrawal or redeployment, but, more importantly, the administration did little to undertake the sort of reorganization or expansion that would be necessary to meet the challenges of what came to be called "the long war." Inside the Department of Defense—and even as the prospects for an early reduction in troop levels in Afghanistan and Iraq vanished—the focus on technological transformation, on self-referential capabilities, and on strategic mobility and access returned. Ironically, Andrew Krepinevich, one of the earliest and most insightful of the transformationists and a former member of the National Defense Panel, understood what few other strategists could not—or chose not to—grasp. In his 2003 first-blush assessment of Operation Iraqi Freedom, Krepinevich wrote,

> If there was ever any doubt that the United States is in the regime-change business, the Second Gulf War should dispel it. Since the fall of the Berlin Wall, the United States has, directly or indirectly, deposed the regime of a foreign state roughly once every three years. But those who practice regime change incur certain responsibilities as well as moral and political consequences. The United States must stabilize Iraq, lest it incur a significant setback in its efforts to make progress in the war against hostile Islamic regimes and radical Islamic terrorist organizations. Success, however, will likely involve a protracted occupation of Islamic states and extract substantial human and material costs. This means the U.S. military's preference to do what it does best—defeat enemy forces in the field and then quickly

depart—must be overcome. The practice of crafting quick exit strategies must yield to a willingness to develop a comprehensive strategy for winning both the war and the post-conflict period that follows. In short, the American military—the Army, in particular—must create a significant capability for conducting stability operations.[31]

The Defense Department's response to these new tasks has been inadequate. While the Army and Marine Corps have worked assiduously to meet the demands of irregular warfare by shifting tactics and reshaping training, the administration has refused to expand the force. Secretary Rumsfeld once lamented that there was no choice but to "go to war with the army you have, not the army you might want or wish to have."[32] But that is no excuse for choosing to remain with essentially the same sized force year after year. In fact, the overall readiness of the Army has fallen as the war has continued. All Army units not deployed or immediately preparing to deploy have "C-4" readiness ratings, the lowest rating possible. This somewhat arcane bureaucratic measure expresses a very profound reality: U.S. ground forces are stretched to the point where they will be unable to respond to a new crisis in a timely fashion.[33] Nor has equipment lost either from combat or simple wear and tear been adequately replaced.[34]

The 2006 edition of the Quadrennial Defense Review does nothing to redress these fundamental contradictions of American policy. Particularly unsatisfying is the review's discussion of the requirements for the long war in the greater Middle East, the conflict central to the Bush Doctrine. The Defense Department's model and preferred scenario is a potted history of Afghanistan—the QDR features pictures of special operations forces on horseback—that distorts the lessons for U.S. forces. First, in this telling, there was the invasion, which "reinforced the principles of adaptability, speed of action, integrated joint operations, economy of force, and the value of working with and through indigenous forces."[35] Since then, as the report would have it, the reconstruction and counterinsurgency campaigns have been the mission of the NATO-led International Security Assistance Force of 9,000 troops. There is no mention of the long-term U.S. force presence that has averaged about 18,000 troops and surged, at election and other crucial times, above 20,000. The QDR prefers to regard this as a temporary, transitory mission.

The telling of the Iraq story is similarly distorted: "The weight of effort in Iraq has shifted over time, from defeating the Iraqi military and liberating the Iraqi people, to building up Iraqi security forces and local institutions, and to transitioning responsibility for security to the Iraqis."[36] What about the continuing counterinsurgency role of U.S. forces? Or their emerging mission to forestall a larger civil war and help disarm and demobilize sectarian militias? Again, the QDR does not adequately address the long-term implications of what President Bush has described as the central front in the long war in the greater Middle East.[37] The report, in essence, ignores the obvious demands that will fall on the military that flow from the president's broad plans for reshaping the Middle East. As a nation, we have made it clear we will no longer risk ignoring states that harbor or support terrorists and who, themselves, are attempting to acquire weapons of mass destruction. But, as one might expect, those states and their allies are fighting back, and there will be no quick solution. Planning a defense posture that ignores that fact puts the country at risk. As Teddy Roosevelt noted more than a century ago, "Unreadiness for war is merely rendered more disastrous by readiness to bluster; to talk defiance and advocate a vigorous policy in words, while refusing to back up these words by deeds."[38]

The 5 Percent Solution

The collapse of the Soviet Union inevitably gave rise to calls to cut America's Cold War force structure. And throughout the 1990s, that is precisely what happened. But these cuts were based on the misleading premise that the active-duty forces of the early 1990s were the same forces America would have gone to war with against the Soviet Union and its allies. In reality, America's active-duty forces were stationed around the world to buy time until the United States and its allies could marshal the additional hundreds of thousands of reserve forces needed to conduct the actual war. The force of the early '90s was, in effect, America's global placeholder, deterring threats in key regions of the world and reassuring allied states that the United States would be there should a conflict erupt. These tasks remain; hence, the decision to cut U.S. force structure since then has made it increasingly difficult to provide this necessary global presence, especially when combined with the fact that the American military has been asked to take on mission after mission since the Cold War's end.[39]

Of course, in theory, as a nation, we could have said "no" to all or most of those missions. Yet, one of the most striking facts of the post–Cold War era has been that while both the Clinton and Bush administrations entered office determined to have America play a less active day-to-day role on the world stage, they left or will leave office having accepted the same basic fact of international life: In the absence of an effective system of global governance, the United States will inevitably be left with the primary responsibility to keep the peace in regions of the world we think are of vital interest. Moreover, doing so means we will also be in the crosshairs of those whose own agenda we frustrate by playing that role, requiring in turn a commitment on our part to deter and, if necessary, confront them militarily. In short, while many have suggested that the United States undertake fewer commitments overseas, the logic of the international system is such that no administration—Democrat or Republican—has seen fit to stem the demand for U.S. forces. Though it may wish to subscribe to the sentiment expressed in the title of the old Broadway play, *Stop the World—I Want to Get Off*, the United States can't.

When it comes to providing adequate resources for our military, however, we seem to act as though it were possible. Beginning in the early 1990s, Washington dug a hole for the military that the services have yet to climb out of. If one compares, for example, the final defense plan put forward by George H. W. Bush's administration in 1992 for the FYDP (Future Years Defense Program) with what the Clinton administration actually spent over those same six years, the net reduction totals $162 billion. Although Congress added through budget amendments and supplemental spending bills $50 billion to the Clinton administration requests, most of the additions went to covering shortfalls in operations and readiness. What these added funds did not "buy back" was the administration's deferred procurement of weapons or its cuts in active-duty personnel. Indeed, the Clinton administration's FY 2001 budget was the first to fulfill its own stated goal of providing $60 billion for new equipment and systems—a goal that had been set years before.[40] In other words, even by the Clinton Pentagon's own measure, the procurement deficit was approaching $70 billion.[41] Others placed the figure higher. For example, the Joint Chiefs had put the bottom line figure for procurement at $75 billion a year.[42] In 2000, the Congressional Budget Office (CBO) was arguing that some $90 billion was needed annually just to maintain a steady rate of procurement for the forces then in place.[43] To take but one service, according to the Army, by 2001 it was some $50 billion in the hole when it came to buying needed equipment.[44]

Given its rhetoric about help being on the way, one might have expected the George W. Bush team to have increased procurement spending substantially. It didn't. If the CBO estimate is taken as a baseline, the additional shortfall in spending now totals an additional $100 billion. And even for FY 2007, the defense procurement budget remains at just over $84 billion, below the $90 billion target suggested by the CBO. Add in inflation since that target figure was set and new monies set aside for missile defense, and the gap is even more substantial.

But how can this be, an average citizen may ask? Hasn't defense spending shot up over the past five years? The short answer is yes. But most of the increase has gone to pay for military personnel costs and operations and maintenance tied to the wars in Iraq and Afghanistan. Between FYs 2000 and 2007, procurement spending went from $55 billion to $84 billion; an increase to be sure, but one entirely inadequate for keeping up with the recapitalization of the military. Moreover, the problem will only get worse as the equipment being used in Iraq and Afghanistan wears out faster than it would in peacetime. Core defense spending is not rising as much as one might have expected. As Krepinevich, now executive director of the Center for Strategic and Budgetary Assessments, has noted, America's military buildup has been "a hollow buildup," filled with funds for operations, maintenance, readiness, and health care—but not systems acquisitions.[45]

Nor has there been much relief on the personnel front. From 1989 to 1999, military end strength was cut from 2.1 million to 1.4 million. For the Army in particular, this meant a dramatic reduction in the number of divisions—from eighteen to ten. As early as 1997, the House Armed Services Committee reported that the Army was being worn down by repeated deployments, and that readiness levels were low and getting lower. With two major wars, stabilization, counterterrorism, and counterinsurgency operations thrown in, the marginal increase in Army manpower (approximately 30,000) in recent years is not much more than a band-aid for what ails America's ground forces. Indeed, the increase itself was only initially intended as a temporary measure, designed to help ease the burden of reorganizing the field army into "modular," brigade-sized units. The relentless manpower needs of Iraq deployments have simply been assumed away—the current budget plan calls for a further reduction in Marine strength of 5,000, even as the Corps recalls members of its individual "ready reserve" back to active duty.

If the government's projected budgets hold true, the recapitalization problems we face will only get worse in the years ahead. According to the Office of Management and Budget (OMB), defense spending is expected to decline from 4.1 percent of GDP in 2006 to 3.1 percent in 2011. Because of the deferments in procurement from the early 1990s on, there is a planned wave of new systems and platforms coming online in the years ahead to replace and upgrade worn-out and out-of-date equipment; however, this "procurement bow wave" cannot possibly be met under current spending plans.[46] It is inevitable, then, that the American military will shrink in materiel and men unless its budget is increased; in turn, the gap between what our national security strategy calls for and what the men and women of the U.S. military are able to provide will continue to grow.

Although the defense budget has increased, the core budget, which excludes the supplemental appropriations passed each year to pay for operations in Iraq and Afghanistan, has grown by just over 20 percent when adjusted for inflation. And a considerable amount of that increase has gone to the pay and benefits associated with the all-volunteer force. The Pentagon is not breaking the nation's bank. The fact is, relative to the economy and the federal budget, the military's share has been on the decline. In FY 1991 national defense expenditures accounted for over 20 percent of federal outlays; in FY 2011, they are expected to account for just 16 percent.

Despite the fact that the country is at war, defense spending as a percentage of the national economy remains low relative to any set of years since World War II. Hence, as has been noted by Lawrence Lindsey, the former chairman of the president's Council of Economic Advisers, the U.S. economy is more than able to handle what needs to be spent on defense. Moreover, that cost, like any investment, should be calculated based on the benefits it brings: Success in Iraq, defeat of the global jihadists, and deterrence of other states from breaking the peace would be an immense return on dollars spent.[47] Dedicating 5 percent of the country's GDP—a nickel on the dollar—to defense is a wise investment.

Winning in Iraq and Afghanistan, winning the global war on terror, having the arms and men to react to a new crisis—whether with Iran, North Korea, or an imploding Pakistan—and preparing the military to hedge against a rising China that may be more ambitious than peaceful are all tasks the United States and its military will be confronted with for some time to come. Attempting to carry out those missions on the cheap invites disaster, and may well end up being far more costly than the increased spending necessary to tackle each of these missions effectively. Numbers have always mattered. They still do.

2

Protracted Wars and the Army's Future

Frederick W. Kagan

In 1986, Charles Heller and William Stofft published a book entitled *America's First Battles* that explored why U.S. forces had lost the first major battle of every war between 1776 and 1965.[1] The thesis, part of a larger argument motivating transformation of the U.S. Army in the 1970s and 1980s, was that future wars would be short, sharp affairs in which such a performance would lead not to subsequent rebirth and triumph but to rapid defeat. A similar book written today about the military struggles of the past two decades might be called instead *America's Long Wars*. From 1989 to the present, the U.S. military has proved remarkably adept at winning the first battle of each war, but has then found itself bogged down in a series of protracted conflicts for which it was unprepared. Winning the first battle is clearly still important, but it is no longer enough, if it ever was. The challenge before the American military today is shaping a force that can win "rapidly and decisively," to use the Pentagon's pet phrase, but can also convert military success into political victory, however long that may take. Success or failure in this effort will turn largely on the course chosen by the U.S. Army.

Since 1989, U.S. armed forces have removed a drug-lord dictator from Panama, driven Saddam Hussein out of Kuwait, attempted to mitigate a politically controlled famine in Somalia, attempted to mediate the restoration of democracy and stability in Haiti, mediated and then imposed an international resolution of the Bosnian crisis, attempted to prevent "ethnic cleansing" in Kosovo, removed the Taliban from power in Afghanistan, and removed Saddam Hussein from power in Iraq. Of these eight major military operations, five have led to the long-term deployment of significant American forces. Tens of thousands of soldiers, sailors, and airmen patrolled the no-fly zones in Iraq and deterred Saddam from reattempting the conquest of Kuwait throughout the 1990s. The implementation of the Dayton Accords in Bosnia in 1995 required the decade-long deployment of an American brigade combat team. A similar long-term commitment was necessary after a sixty-nine-day 1999 bombing campaign in Kosovo. "Rapid, decisive" operations in Afghanistan in 2001 and Iraq in 2003 have so far required the subsequent deployment of nearly 200,000 soldiers, sailors, airmen, and Marines for years.

Of the three cases not followed by long-term deployments, two were failures. The collapse of will following the "Black Hawk Down" disaster in Somalia led to the complete abandonment of that effort—and the propagation of a host of problems that U.S. Central Command is still nervously tracking (including the recent seizure of Mogadishu by radical Islamist militias and the growing prospect of a wider Somalia-Ethiopia war). The rapid removal of U.S. forces from Haiti permitted the rapid collapse of that settlement as well. Only the removal of Manuel Noriega from control of Panama appears to have proceeded quickly, successfully, and without as much need for a significant long-term U.S. presence.

With the exception of the Iraqi no-fly zones, moreover, the long-term presence required has been heavily weighted toward ground forces—above all, toward the Army. Although Marine units have been heavily engaged in Iraq and, to a lesser extent, Afghanistan, there are simply not enough of them to carry the burden. Moreover, the need to keep a significant number of Marine units ready for the forced-entry missions for which they are prepared has also militated against the lengthy deployments to which the Army has been forced to resort in Iraq and Afghanistan. The nature of current warfare, it seems, demands the ability to deploy significant numbers of Army forces into hostile and semihostile environments for years at a time and in multiple theaters simultaneously. It is difficult to imagine any sound plan for the future of the Army that does not proceed from this reality.

Three questions bedevil efforts to think about that future more concretely: Will the trends of the past two decades continue? Can we replace manpower with technology? Can we substitute indigenous forces for American troops? Until very recently, U.S. national security policy had assumed that the answers to these questions were no, yes, and yes. Emphasis on "shock and awe" and "network-centric operations" explicitly assumed that the "rapid, decisive" destruction of the enemy's military was the primary challenge to be met.[2] Military strategists, both civilian and uniformed, implicitly assumed that the trend toward protracted deployments would ease.[3] They also argued that it would be possible to replace manpower-intensive operations with "smaller footprint" missions "enabled" by advanced technologies. And in the wake of Operation Enduring Freedom in Afghanistan, those advocating reliance on special forces to support indigenous troops, rather than on the use of American forces, received powerful and broad-based support.[4]

The only major change that has resulted from America's experience in Iraq and Afghanistan, as evidenced by the 2006 Quadrennial Defense Review, is the conviction that protracted conflicts may be more the norm. The solutions to this problem proposed in the QDR and by outside analysts have remained the same, however: The use of indigenous forces and technology will offset the apparent impossibility of maintaining sufficient ground forces to conduct such operations on a large scale with American troops. In other words, although recent analysis has corrected a major disconnect between previous strategies and the reality of common American long-term deployments, it has only reinforced the preference for these same two solutions.

This preference is extremely problematic, however, relying as it does on a number of generic assumptions that may well fail in any particular case. As a result, the QDR and most subsequent defense commentary still dramatically underestimate the actual requirement for ground forces, wishing the problem onto optimistic solutions that past experience (and all reason) suggest may not be available.

There is also an elephant in the room that discussions about future force requirements rarely acknowledge: the high cost of resetting the Army in the wake of operations in Iraq. This is a worrisome part of the ground forces equation. The ground forces are stretched today in part because they were inadequately maintained and starved of resources in the 1990s. The heavy use of military equipment in Iraq and Afghanistan will require a significant recapitalization program just to bring the force back to levels that have already proved inadequate for current needs. If this program is not factored into future plans that also include a significant expansion of the ground forces, the result will be to wish on the next administration an even larger deficit in military capability than President George W. Bush inherited in 2001.

Assumptions

Military planning during Donald Rumsfeld's terms as secretary of defense rested on three basic assumptions about the nature of future conflict: Future wars will be short, sharp affairs; their outcomes will turn heavily on the opponents' relative levels of technology; and the United States can and should rely increasingly on using indigenous forces instead of its own ground troops. All three assumptions have been badly undermined by recent operations (and, indeed, not-so-recent operations, as well), and analysts and policymakers are increasingly coming to question them. If secretary-designate Robert M. Gates rejects or modifies them, as he should, then the course of U.S. military planning will change radically.

The Length of Future Conflicts. Most major military conflicts the United States has won have required significant long-term troop deployments to stabilize and maintain the subsequent peace settlements. Thus, the post–Civil War period saw the protracted deployment of the Army in Reconstruction. U.S. forces remained in Germany and Japan for several years following World War II, establishing and stabilizing the peace settlements there—and then lingered for almost five more decades to secure those settlements against a power that, it was feared, would seek to revise them. American troops have remained in Korea since the 1953 ceasefire for the same reason.

Nor is this tendency toward protracted peace-enforcement missions uniquely American. Coalition forces remained in France for several years after 1815 to ensure the stability of the Vienna settlement. British and French forces remained in Germany for a considerable time after World War I to enforce the Versailles Treaty. And British forces remained in various garrisons throughout the Middle East for decades to stabilize the results of the peace settlements that broke up the Ottoman Empire. Long-term deployments do not necessarily lead to successful peace settlements, but successful peace settlements seem frequently to require long-term deployments.

There are certainly some conflicts one could imagine in the future that would not lead to such a requirement. A Chinese attack on Taiwan blunted by U.S. air and sea forces might well lead to a return to the status quo without a significant change in deployment patterns. Small-scale operations to remove unacceptable leaders, as in the case of Grenada in 1983, in areas not otherwise of major concern might also conceivably end quickly. But most other likely military operations will probably require significant deployments to establish and support an acceptable peace settlement. This is to say nothing of peacekeeping, peace-enforcement, and humanitarian assistance operations, which are normally of long duration by their very nature.

The possibility of conflict with Iran provides an illuminating example of the challenges the U.S. military might face. Even the prospect of a land war against Iran is unsettling, to say nothing of the difficulty of establishing and enforcing a peace settlement. Iran is roughly four times as large as Iraq, with nearly three times the population. In contrast to Iraq's relatively flat and featureless terrain, Iran has significant mountainous areas and relatively few broad plains. Historically based calculations of the occupation forces required for Iraq have suggested the need for around 250,000 troops (although the coalition has never had that many soldiers there). Similar calculations for Iran would call for hundreds of thousands more.[5] There are fewer than 500,000 troops in the active Army today. The prospect is, indeed, daunting.

While the current crisis over Iran's nuclear program may well be defused peacefully, either through diplomatic efforts or through a change in the course of the Iranian regime, it is not possible simply to decide that military action against Iran will not be required. Iran's nuclear program seems already to be sufficiently advanced that, in the absence of a complete Iranian surrender, a partial settlement in the near future may lead to the resurrection of a similar crisis down the road. This has been the pattern in both Iraq after 1991 and North Korea since the 1980s: Partially defused crises reemerge periodically because the offending state never completely surrendered to full international monitoring and control. If this pattern is repeated long enough, or if the Iranian regime does actually approach the stage at which it could develop a usable nuclear weapon, an international crisis is likely to ensue that could well trigger military action in response to any of several possible scenarios.

Military action against Iran might be restricted to airstrikes against known or suspected nuclear sites, but such operations are unlikely to result in a permanent resolution of the crisis, either. Some of Iran's nuclear sites are thought to be deeply buried, and it is not clear that the United States and its allies have a complete picture of the Iranian nuclear program. It will be difficult, therefore, to verify that the program has been completely destroyed without imposing a strict monitoring regime on the Iranians. If they continue to defy international inspections in the wake of an airstrike, the likelihood is that the crisis will continue, possibly after a pause of longer or shorter duration. Once again, the model of Iraq in the 1990s is informative here: Periodic airstrikes, culminating in the large-scale missile campaign in 1998 dubbed Operation Desert Fox, did not suffice to convince international monitors or the international community that the danger had passed. The long-term resolution of the Iranian nuclear crisis may well require, therefore, the deposition of the current regime and the occupation of all or part of the country. The need to have the capability to perform such an operation is likely to be a long-term one.

From the standpoint of current probable operations, Iran is the long-pole in the tent. Although the North Korean military is nominally larger, its actual combat power is open to serious question, and the South Korean ground forces are strong and substantial.

North Korea, moreover, is about one-fourth the size of Iraq, with about the same population. Scenarios for possible intervention in North Korea are as complex as they are improbable in the short term, but none is likely to require a commitment of American ground forces remotely on a par with what might be needed in Iran.

The prospect of the collapse of the Pakistani government and the need to control the 125 million Pakistanis and their nuclear weapons is nightmarish. It is also unlikely. Pervez Musharraf may well fall from power one way or the other, but it is by no means clear that Pakistan will thereupon either fall apart or take any sort of action that will require the United States to occupy it. As the basis for force-planning, it would not make sense to insist upon the creation of ground forces able to undertake such a mission, although force-planners should have it in the corners of their eyes as they consider worst-case scenarios. Additionally, one might imagine crises in Indonesia, Brazil, or other large and heavily populated lands, but none of these is sufficiently probable to serve as a useful scenario for shaping the size of the Army.

Considering the problem of Iran first and foremost, then, is not merely focusing on the problem of the moment. It is focusing on a clear and present danger that also presents the largest challenge among scenarios likely to emerge within the planning horizon of current force-structure debates. Creating forces capable of allowing the United States to contemplate major operations in Iran, moreover, will also mean creating forces with sufficient capabilities to allow contemplation of several smaller, simultaneous deployments with much greater equanimity than is possible with today's military. Adequately sized U.S. ground forces should have been able to undertake the mission of pacifying Iraq without suffering as great a strain as they have.

A variety of arguments suggest the need for forces somewhat smaller than the several hundred thousand suggested above to establish a tolerable regime in Iran in the wake of a major military operation. Iran is a more urbanized and homogeneous society than Iraq. Deposing and replacing the current government, which is neither broadly popular nor remotely as totalitarian as Saddam

Hussein's state, should not call forth serious internal ethnic strife, although the danger of a more unified insurgency against the occupying forces is more significant than it was in Iraq. It is certainly not a mission the United States could easily contemplate without allies, moreover, and the news on that front is somewhat mixed—although both Britain and France, the only two European states with sizable and deployable ground forces, have been supportive of efforts to curb Iran's nuclear program, the steps they would ultimately be willing to take to stop that program remain unclear.

Even so, it is hard to imagine contemplating an operation in Iran responsibly without the availability of several times as many American ground forces as are now in Iraq. In the context of the current discussions about Iraq, such a number seems absurd. It is not. In 1990 and 1991, the United States and its allies deployed 650,000 troops to the Persian Gulf. The surge at that level lasted less than a year, so the problem of rotating forces through the theater was mitigated, and maintaining force levels near that size for a longer term would certainly have strained the U.S. military of the time very badly; but it could probably have been managed, if necessary. An increase in the size of the active Army back to the level sustained throughout the 1980s—around 750,000—together with a significant mobilization of the National Guard and Reserves (which did not occur in 1990–91 for a variety of reasons) would make it possible to contemplate adequate postwar force ratios in Iran if necessary, although with considerable pain. The question is not whether the United States could field a force large enough to handle such a challenging mission, but whether there is a way to solve the problem at a lower cost.

Technology. The American military was cut from its Cold War structure to its present size after 1991 on the basis of two arguments. First, the collapse of the Soviet Union and the destruction of Saddam Hussein's army seemed to remove any meaningful threat for the foreseeable future (the United States was said to have entered a "strategic pause"). Second, new technologies showcased on a large scale for the first time in the Gulf War were said to promise dramatic reductions in the size of the ground forces needed to win future wars. The days of vast fleets of tanks rolling across the desert were over, it was said. Neither argument has proved to be true.

The "strategic pause" ended on September 11, 2001—if, indeed, it ever really existed. It is no longer possible to argue that the United States does not face any threats in the short- or mid-term, or that it is unnecessary for the military to be prepared for conflict today and tomorrow. This is true even apart from the ongoing wars in Iraq and Afghanistan. Responsible leaders cannot claim that the United States can cash in on any "peace dividend" in order to reprogram money to more urgent domestic needs. Maintaining adequate armed forces for the troubled times ahead has become one of the most urgent requirements of sound government.

The promise that advanced technology would reduce the need for large ground forces, first promoted to greatest effect by President Bill Clinton's first secretary of defense, Les Aspin, has also failed. It failed not so much because it was wrong within the narrow remit of the problems then being considered, as because those problems have proved to be only a small part of the greater challenge facing American armed forces today. Advances in precision-guided munitions and the systems to identify, track, and designate targets for them have certainly reduced the size of ground forces needed simply to defeat an enemy's military. And while it is easy to argue that the Iraqi army of 2003 had been seriously weakened by the first Gulf War and the decade of sanctions and periodic attacks that followed, or that the Taliban had never had significant combat power of the sort that might pose a challenge to conventional forces, the fact remains that improvements in the lethality of the American military between 1991 and 2001 certainly facilitated the more rapid and complete destruction of those militaries than would have been possible previously.[6]

But the conflicts in Iraq and Afghanistan have shown that the destruction of the enemy's military is only the prelude to the real operations that will determine the success or failure of the undertaking—operations designed to establish and secure the peace and enable an orderly transition to the new regimes that will sustain it. In these operations, it has become clear, the technology of American forces is not enough to compensate for reduced troop deployments. This argument, developed in greater detail elsewhere, rests on the simple fact that most of the technologies that have received the greatest emphasis in the past decade and a half are devoted to destroying things and killing people. But the task of generating useful intelligence about the political, economic, and social developments that are key to success in postcombat operations can only be accomplished by human beings. Tasks such as crowd control, police functions, and the training of indigenous forces and police cannot be replicated by machines. Air theorists began to argue in the 1990s that airpower could actually control territory. That is true, if the means of control can be restricted to terror, and the method can be pure destruction. Such techniques will not succeed in the complex and delicate situations that follow the ends of most major wars, and so the promise of technology is unlikely to mitigate the need for large numbers of ground troops any time soon.[7]

Indigenous Forces. Challenged by the need to face wars such as those in Iraq, Afghanistan, and maybe even Iran in the new defense environment, some experts have begun to declare that the "traditional" methods relying on the use of American forces are simply untenable today. "There is an easier way," they sometimes declare— that is, the preparation, support, and use of indigenous forces in place of Americans. This argument surfaced prominently in the wake of the attack against Afghanistan in 2001, with many arguing that that conflict would usher in a new way of warfare: American Special Forces teams would cooperate with local fighters, avoiding the need for U.S. combat troops. With all the strain placed on U.S. forces to support operations in Iraq—and with the much greater strain operations in Iran would impose in prospect—this example is coming to the fore once again.

By contrast with the argument that technology will solve America's military problems, the claims for the role of indigenous forces are much more meaningful. In almost any postconflict security operation, success will only come when indigenous military and police forces are willing and able to take continued responsibility for maintaining order and supporting a government that will enforce the terms of the peace. Preparing and training indigenous forces is definitely a precondition for success.

The argument that relying on indigenous forces from the outset could reduce the number of American troops needed, however, is far less convincing. It is not possible to train adequate numbers of indigenous forces before operations commence. It is not safe to rely on already existing indigenous forces to enforce a peace many of them are likely to oppose. And it is not acceptable to allow a lengthy period of disorder following the end of major combat operations while training indigenous forces in-country. Relying on indigenous forces instead of American and allied troops risks Iraq-like disasters.

A country the size of Iraq requires several hundred thousand soldiers and police to reestablish order following the destruction of the ruling government and then to maintain that order during the transition to a new form of polity. It is out of the question to spirit hundreds of thousands of, say, Iranians out of Iran, train them somewhere else, and reinsert them into the country after the fall of the regime. Efforts to do something like this prior to the Iraq invasion produced a laughably small result not because they were poorly executed, but because the task itself was not merely impossible, but ridiculous. Military operations have to start and finish before the United States and its allies can begin the process of preparing and training indigenous forces on a meaningful scale.

In Afghanistan, the United States relied on indigenous forces already in existence, notably the Northern Alliance, but also a number of Pashtun tribes. Many have argued that the Iraqi army could have been used in a similar role had it not been prematurely disbanded. No doubt one could scour Iran for military and paramilitary forces that could conceivably be co-opted and used to establish and maintain order. This approach is as unlikely to lead to success as attempting to train indigenous forces in advance of an operation, however. It worked in Afghanistan because the country was still in the throes of civil war, with the Northern Alliance troops on which the United States relied actively engaged in fighting the government the United States sought to depose. No such situation held in totalitarian Iraq, and no such situation holds in largely peaceful and stable Iran. In both of those states—and in North Korea and most other potential foes as well—the government really does hold a monopoly of force, as governments normally do. Any military, police, or paramilitary forces in the country are therefore controlled by the government and are sufficiently loyal to it that they do not present any threat to it now. They are exceedingly unlikely to be stable and reliable allies in an effort to depose that government and establish a new order from which its friends and supporters are almost certain to be excluded. Whatever the wisdom of simply disbanding the Iraqi army from the standpoint of fueling the insurgency, it was not a foolish decision for the reason that it deprived the coalition of forces that could reliably have been used to maintain order. It could never have served that function, and neither could the military or police of Iran or North Korea.[8]

If indigenous forces are to be used, therefore, they can only be new formations developed after the end of major combat operations. U.S. strategy can be more or less sophisticated in allowing members of the former military and police forces into the new bodies, and the wisdom of such decisions will depend heavily on specific circumstances. But the creation of usable military and police units will rely on training by American and coalition troops after the government has fallen.

Such training had long been a Special Forces task, but Iraq and Afghanistan have both revealed that the scale of the requirement for trainers is far beyond what the Special Forces can support. In the future, all ground forces units must be prepared to serve as military advisers and trainers to help ready indigenous forces to replace them. Even with such a change in mission, the U.S. military will find that it still takes considerable time to form new indigenous forces. Months of training will be required even in the most optimistic scenarios (those in which units are composed of former police or military personnel with considerable training and reliable loyalties, for example). There is simply a minimum period of time required to form and train any military or police unit to basic competence. Since the training mission will need the support of a substantial number of U.S. and coalition forces if it is to proceed rapidly, there will be a significant period in which many U.S. troops and almost all indigenous forces are engaged not in maintaining order or resisting budding insurgencies, but in training.[9]

If the United States sends inadequate numbers of ground troops to begin with, this period will almost certainly result in the collapse of civil order, the growth of criminality and violence, and the burgeoning of insurgent movements that aim to thwart the establishment of a new order conducive to U.S. and coalition interests.[10] As we have seen repeatedly in Iraq, Afghanistan, and elsewhere, it is much more difficult for a nascent government to fight an insurgency that has been allowed to take root than it would have been to prevent it from establishing itself to begin with. Politics abhors a vacuum. If the new government is incapable of establishing security, and American and coalition forces do not do so, then groups opposed to the coalition's interests will step into the breach in the guise of maintaining security themselves. Failure to establish and maintain order from the moment the bullets stop flying in any given area is an invitation to disorder and insurgency. Reliance on indigenous forces to justify smaller-than-necessary U.S. troop levels is likely to guarantee a repetition of the sorts of problems the United States has encountered in Iraq.

Is it proposed, then, to prepare the U.S. Army to fight the last war better? Yes, because the last war highlighted truths and problems that had been visible in many previous struggles. As we have seen, the majority of America's wars have required the protracted deployment of troops to secure the peace. Many have required the establishment of indigenous forces to replace those that had been shattered in the struggle or dissolved with the old regime. The American military has encountered each repetition of this requirement as though it were a new problem, has done very little until the past few years to develop meaningful doctrine, and has largely wished that each such experience would be the last. It is time finally to internalize this basic lesson about the nature of war termination and prepare the Army to fight the last war, a series of previous wars, and many likely wars of the future.

Numbers Matter

The number of soldiers in the U.S. Army, both active and reserve, will continue to be a critical determinant of America's ability to win future wars and, above all, the peaces that follow them. The current force is far too small. It was cut after the end of the Cold War on the basis of optimistic assumptions that have proved invalid. A hard look at the most challenging likely near- and mid-term threats suggests that the Cold War force level was about right. The active Army should consist of about 750,000 troops, with the Army Reserves and National Guard at about the current level. Forces smaller than these place America's national security fundamentally in jeopardy.

It will immediately be objected that it is impossible to recruit such a force without resorting to conscription. If that objection were valid, it would be fatal. Converting today's volunteer military into a conscript force would result in a dramatic degradation of its effectiveness and professionalism, seriously reducing its competence in precisely the areas most urgently required in postcombat operations—policing, training of indigenous forces, and counterinsurgency operations. It is impossible, moreover, to imagine a system of conscription that is remotely fair. More than two million young men reach military age in America each year. Supporting an Army of a reasonable size would mean drafting only a small percentage of them, inevitably generating the same feelings regarding draft "winners" and draft "losers" that led to the elimination of conscription in the 1970s. Without a major war of national mobilization, conscription is not an option.

It is also not necessary. The United States maintained an active Army of between 770,000 and 780,000 continually between 1974 and 1989 entirely through voluntary accessions. That period covers recessions and economic booms, the hottest period of the Cold War, and the period of *perestroika* leading to the fall of the Berlin Wall and the collapse of the Soviet Union. It includes periods of expansion in the eighteen- to twenty-one-year-old population and periods of contraction in that population. Problems in recruiting bedeviled efforts in the early 1980s, but were offset by aggressive and successful national programs to make the military more attractive to potential recruits. It is true that this period of stable and larger forces did not see a significant counterinsurgency campaign, a problem that has led to difficulties in recruiting even the smaller force of today. It is very likely, however, that the period of a very large American deployment will come to an end within a few years, either in success or in failure. And the memory of conscription and defeat in Vietnam did not prevent the Army from recruiting to its goal of 780,000 even in the years immediately following the U.S. withdrawal. If the president and congressional leaders make a call to national service and attractive incentives are put into place, there is no reason to imagine that the Army cannot recruit to a larger end strength over the next several years.

The process of expanding the active Army will certainly be expensive. In addition to whatever funds are required to support recruiting incentives and advertising, the cost of military manpower has soared in recent years as the result of much-needed improvements in military quality of life and health care, and it will be necessary to purchase or refurbish equipment sets for the new units, as well as support their annual operations and maintenance costs.

The total cost of expanding the active Army to the level of 750,000 or so will probably be in the vicinity of an additional $33 billion per year in fixed personnel and operations and maintenance costs (once the units have all been recruited and fielded), with another $60 billion or so required to purchase the equipment for the new units.[11] If this program were executed over five years, the average annual cost would come to something like $45 billion. That would be an increase of about 40 percent over the baseline FY 2007 defense budget, or about 30 percent over the FY 2006 budget, including the supplementals. Once the fixed costs for purchasing brigade equipment sets were met, the recurring annual cost of about $33 billion would constitute a little under 30 percent of the baseline FY 2007 defense budget.

Whether or not the active Army expands, however, it will still be necessary to enlarge the Army's budget just to bring the force back to the level of capability it had before March 2003. Operations in Iraq and Afghanistan have played havoc with the Army's equipment. Tanks normally rated to drive a few hundred miles in a year have been driven over five thousand. Helicopters have operated continuously and in extremely harsh conditions. The Iraqi sand has taken a heavy toll on the Army's rotary-wing fleet, as well as its fleet of trucks and Humvees. The nature of the war has also imposed a higher cost on the Army's equipment than a conventional war would have done, since the insurgents have attacked unarmed and unarmored vehicles that would not normally be expected to see combat. Shot-up Humvees and trucks must be repaired or replaced; Humvees weighed down with bolted-on armor must be refurbished. Everything from communications equipment filled with sand to tents and dented canteens must be brought back up to acceptable specifications. Estimates from the Army and outside analysts suggest that the price tag will be about $9 billion per year for each year the war in Iraq continues—and then for at least two years after it has ended. This temporary increase in the Army's budget is nonnegotiable if America is to have a battleworthy ground force after the Iraq war.[12]

The need for these budget increases comes at an awkward time for the Army, which had been focusing on two modernization programs expected to cost $220 billion or more over the next several years: modularity and the Future Combat System. The modularity program is a reorganization of the Army's basic fighting units—divisions, brigades, and battalions. Put briefly, the Army will move from a structure in which most divisions had three brigades, each with three maneuver battalions, to one in which a division will have four brigades, each with two maneuver battalions and one reconnaissance, surveillance, and target-acquisition (RSTA, pronounced Rista) squadron. The main purpose of this reorganization is to make individual brigades more readily deployable. In the past, deploying a brigade meant also deploying vital elements of the divisional, and even corps, logistics structure. This situation is what made the deployment of very small numbers of brigades into the Balkans in the

1990s painful for the Army. Modularity would reduce the problem by increasing the amount of logistical support organic to the brigades.

The modularity program raises a number of concerns. In particular, evidence from the major combat portion of Operation Iraqi Freedom suggests that RSTA squadrons equipped primarily with light vehicles (Humvees and Bradleys, but no tanks) may not perform their designated role of finding and tracking the enemy. Commanders in Operation Iraqi Freedom frequently deployed lightly armed reconnaissance units behind their advancing armored main bodies for fear of losing their thin-skinned scouts to unexpected contact with the enemy. The particular design of these units in the modularity program may require revision. Another problem is the reduction of maneuver battalions in brigade combat teams from three to two. In combat operations, it is customary to maintain a reserve in case of unanticipated contact or stronger-than-expected enemy resistance. A triangular brigade normally moves with two battalions forward and one back—one third of its combat power is an adequate, but not excessive, reserve. Brigades with only two battalions will have either to travel line abreast with no reserve, in column with half of their combat power in reserve, or with the battalions broken up in some other fashion. The increase in Army end strength proposed above could mitigate this problem by filling out the modular brigades to three maneuver battalions each.

Whatever the flaws of the modularity program, the basic concept is fundamentally sound. The Army must be able to deploy individual brigades or small groups of brigades taken from different divisions without degrading the combat capabilities of their sister brigades. Improvements in communications, targeting, and precision-strike capabilities incorporated into the modular brigade program are also important in maintaining the Army's edge in conventional combat operations. Considering that the Army is well along in the conversion of its units to the modular design, moreover, it would be foolish to abandon or significantly reduce or delay the program, even despite its remaining $45 billion price tag.

The major modernization program in the Army, however, is the development and fielding of the Future Combat System. First put in train by General Eric Shinseki in the late 1990s, this program aims to field an integrated group of vehicles and weapons systems that are both light and lethal. The major objective of the FCS program is to harness information technology to improve the Army's ability to identify, track, target, and destroy the enemy at standoff distances. In addition, the program addresses a problem the Army has faced since the 1980s: M1 tanks weigh eighty tons and are very difficult to deploy rapidly. Initially, programmatic materials suggested that the FCS would trade weight for lethality; the program's vehicles were supposed to be able to survive by locating and destroying potential threats before they themselves came within range of the enemy's weapons. Although subsequent developments have increased the survivability of the system and mitigated this reliance on shooting first to kill first, the major vehicles of the family remain less well-armored than the frontal slope of the M1. They are, on the other hand, much lighter and therefore much more readily deployable rapidly by air. They are also considerably more fuel-efficient than the gas-guzzling M1 tank, reducing the logistics burden necessary to maintain them in the field. This improvement will be a significant advantage in both conventional and unconventional warfare.

It is highly questionable, however, whether the entire Army vehicle fleet really needs to be able to fit into a C-130 transport as the original specifications required, and it is even more questionable whether the Army can do without any vehicle that has passive protection greater than the M1 currently provides. Once again, in light of the experience of both the combat and the postcombat phases of Iraq, it seems very likely that the FCS program will have to undergo significant changes in order to provide the Army with the vehicles it will need to triumph in future conflicts. Continuing with the program in some modified form, however, is valuable. The current Army's vehicle fleet design is now three decades old. Enemies have studied it in detail and will develop methods by which to defeat it. Although ingenuity has found ways of incorporating information technology into 1970s chassis, purpose-built systems will do it better. If the disdain for passive armor protection were to give way to an aggressive materials development program to create cost-effective lightweight armor, the results could be as revolutionary for future wars as the M1's capabilities were for previous conflicts. Despite its high price tag—some $160 billion according to recent Government Accountability Office (GAO) estimates—the FCS is worth pursuing.

It is not clear, however, that it should continue to receive the degree of funding priority it has had to date. While developing deployable systems that integrate information technology is a desirable goal, it is less pressing than building a force capable of handling visible missions for which the Army is now unprepared, such as dealing with Iran. There is no threat in existence today whose defeat would require the FCS, but there is a threat whose defeat requires a larger Army. Some tradeoffs in the FCS program, therefore, would be desirable to offset the costs of expanding the active Army. The delay might even prove salutary, especially if the program were diverted from its current preoccupation with lightness into efforts to develop new forms of passive protection. The very flexibility of the acquisition program, which is designed to allow technologies to be fielded piecemeal as they become available, should also facilitate delaying some of those acquisitions in favor of a more pressing requirement. Cost savings along these lines will be small, however, compared to the overall cost of enlarging the active Army, and they should not be accepted if they put the modernization of the force at serious risk.

Conclusion

Forty-five billion dollars a year sounds like a lot of money, but it is not. Considered from one perspective, it is 0.36 percent of the 2005 gross domestic product. The Army's budget could be increased by this amount and defense spending would still be consuming a historically low proportion of the national wealth; before the defense cuts of the 1990s, the last time the military consumed such a small proportion of the GDP was 1948—even with the proposed increase included. Even with this expansion of the active Army, the defense budget would still account for less than 20 percent of the federal budget. The military never consumed less than that percentage of the federal budget throughout the Cold War. If the nation really is at war, as the president repeatedly asserts and hundreds of thousands of servicemen and women can attest, then increases of this magnitude should be taken easily in stride rather than being dismissed as unrealistic. They are only unrealistic if we delude ourselves that there is an alternative.

Throughout the 1990s, defense budgets were primarily based on how much the political leadership felt it could spend on a line item that was widely regarded as a luxury rather than a necessity. The military was then left to divide up the resources that the political leadership chose to make available in the belief that any force those resources produced would be adequate in the "strategic pause" that prevailed. This approach to defense budgets will no longer suffice. The United States is not in a strategic pause, and it matters a great deal whether the military is or is not capable of responding to the strategic challenges it faces. In a world as dangerous as the current one, it is unacceptable for any president to forgo missions vital to American security because the armed forces the budgeters have chosen to make available are inadequate. When the reality of the world does not correspond to "political reality," it is political reality that generally loses.

This chapter has not addressed the Army National Guard and Reserves, despite the enormous contribution they have made to operations in Iraq, Afghanistan, and within the continental United States, for two reasons. First, the issues surrounding those services are so complex that they deserve a chapter of their own.[13] Second, they are not the forces of choice for dealing with the protracted deployments described above.

The distinction between reservists and permanent active-duty soldiers is increasingly not one of capability, but of expectation. Reservists join their units to serve their country, and they are willing to risk their lives to do so. They join the Reserves or the Guard instead of the active force because they do not wish to be full-time professional soldiers, moving from deployment to training to deployment. The purpose of maintaining such reserves is to hedge against uncertainty. When unexpected crises occur as the active force is already committed, or when things go unexpectedly badly in a major conflict, then the National Guard and Reserves are the nation's only fallback. Apart from the important role they play in homeland security operations of all varieties, serving as this backstop for the active forces is their primary mission.[14]

The current plan to turn the Guard and Reserves into an operational, rather than a strategic, reserve (that is, incorporating the deployment of their units into regular rotational cycles in ongoing operations), is a bad idea from two perspectives. First, it eliminates the nation's last trained group of soldiers who are able to respond at short notice to disaster. With the end of conscription and the demolition of the systems that would be necessary to reconstitute it rapidly, the commitment of the Guard and Reserves to an operational role means that if things go badly or unexpected crises pop up, the president will either have no forces available or will have to rush hastily trained cannon-fodder into combat. Neither option is acceptable. That is why the nation needs to maintain a trained and ready reserve.

The second problem with committing the Reserves to an operational role is that such a move breaks the nation's contract with reservists. This is not literally true, of course; the Pentagon has the legal right to mobilize reservists and deploy them for as long as necessary. It is morally true, however, that the regular operational deployment of Guardsmen and reservists turns them involuntarily from being part-time soldiers to being full-time soldiers. In times of crisis, such decisions may be necessary. In planning a sound military with an eye on likely force requirements, however, it is unacceptable to count on such a permanent activation of the Reserves.

For these reasons, the program proposed in this chapter directs suggested budget increases into the active force in the expectation that this will take the burden of protracted deployments from the shoulders of those who did not sign up for them. It is not intended to slight the Reserves or to indicate in any way that various proposals from inside and outside the Pentagon to increase the budget of the Guard and Reserves in order to modernize their equipment and upgrade their training should be scrapped or reduced. The

Guard and Reserves can only perform their vital functions if they are properly equipped and resourced.

Another problem with proposing a large-scale increase in the Army budget is that such suggestions invariably meet with demands from the other services for parallel increases in their budgets. Maintaining budgetary parity among the services has been an unwritten political rule for quite some time. It is time to abandon this rule. Army expansion and modernization should not come at the expense of necessary modernization of the Navy and the Air Force, but neither should it fall victim to arbitrary interservice budget politics. If America's strategic requirements require an imbalance in service budget shares, then so be it.

Throughout the 1990s, advocates of increased defense spending had to argue that periods of peace are, historically, merely the time between wars. It is no longer necessary to make such arguments. War has come, and it has found America's gallant military unprepared for all of its challenges. Yet few of the challenges that are so straining the armed forces today are new or even unusual. Arguments for maintaining the course set in the strategic pause of the 1990s, held to by some even during this time of conflict that has exposed so many flawed assumptions, are sounding increasingly threadbare and unconvincing. The "new think" of the late 1990s has become "old think" in this time of protracted land war. It is past time to adjust America's defense priorities and defense budget to account for the timeless realities of war.

3

Age and Indifference Erode U.S. Air Power

Loren Thompson

America's armed forces fare best in the political system when the nation is in danger and the military is performing well. If danger recedes or defeat looms, they can fare very poorly.

That certainly has been the experience of the Air Force during most of its brief history. Success in World War II brought the Air Force independence from the Army, and the primacy of the nuclear strike mission in early Cold War years made the youngest service first among equals in military councils. During the Vietnam War, in contrast, public dissatisfaction with military performance translated into budget cuts and canceled programs.

With the coming of the new millennium, though, the Air Force has faced a different set of circumstances for which there is little precedent. Although the nation definitely senses danger from foreign terrorists, and the Air Force fought well in three successive air campaigns (the Balkans in 1999, Afghanistan in 2001, and Iraq in 2003), the service is not getting the money it needs to modernize. As a result, service leaders fear their capacity to accomplish core missions is increasingly at risk.[1]

It is common for military services to seek more money even when they are thriving, because in the dangerous business of war, no amount of capability is too much. But that is hardly the situation the Air Force faces today. Every major category of air asset is exhibiting signs of age-related stress, and space efforts are in such disarray that there is a real danger the nation may lose coverage in critical missions, such as missile warning and orbital reconnaissance.[2] To make matters worse, even the systems that are in good shape often seem ill-designed for dealing with the kinds of elusive enemies currently of greatest concern.

This isn't the way Air Force leaders thought the new millennium was going to unfold. They were exposed to the same budget cuts and talk of "asymmetric" threats as everyone else in the 1990s, but unlike the other services they finished the decade with a crushing defeat of U.S. enemies in the Balkans. The performance of U.S. air power in Operation Allied Force—the Balkan air war—was so decisive that it led previous skeptics of air power to speculate that the whole character of warfare might be changing.

Partly as a result of this success and partly because it had traditionally been the most technology-intensive of the military services, the Air Force began the third millennium as the perceived favorite of a new crop of political appointees at the Pentagon. Since those appointees, led by Defense Secretary Donald Rumsfeld, were proclaiming their intention to transform the nation's military posture with cutting-edge technology, it seemed likely to many observers that the Air Force was destined once again to be *primus inter pares* in military deliberations.

It didn't work out that way. Although Rumsfeld's inner circle touted the success of precision bombing and space reconnaissance in Afghanistan and Iraq, its members didn't get along with the Air Force's civilian and uniformed leaders. In the 2001 Quadrennial Defense Review, the service rebuffed proposals from the Office of the Secretary of Defense (OSD) to buy more B-2 bombers. In 2002, the secretary of the Air Force, James Roche, threatened to resign over OSD efforts to cut funding for the F-22 fighter. In 2003, OSD and the Air Force secretariat engaged in a bitter dispute over whether future tactical surveillance should be conducted from manned aircraft (as in the past) or from unmanned vehicles and spacecraft. In 2004, the Air Force became embroiled in a procurement scandal that dragged the defense secretary into a confrontation with his own party's most powerful senators.

So by the time President George W. Bush's first term ended, Secretary Rumsfeld and his key advisers had decided the Air Force wasn't their favorite military branch, after all. That honor was reserved for the Department of the Navy, alumni of which soon occupied the deputy secretary's office, the chairmanship and vice chairmanship of the Joint Chiefs of Staff, and the leadership of most of the combatant commands. The Air Force thus approached the 2005 Quadrennial Defense Review with a sense of foreboding, shorn of civilian leaders, and its influence at a low ebb.

Quadrennial Review Neglects Air Power

The basic problem the Air Force confronted in the 2005 quadrennial review was that policymakers and the political system had come to take global air dominance for granted. No American soldier had been killed by hostile military aircraft since the Korean War, and no American pilot had been shot down by enemy aircraft since the Vietnam War. The surprising loss of a first-generation stealth aircraft to Serbian ground fire in the Balkan air war was regarded as an anomaly rather than part of some broader trend, and many policymakers discounted Air Force reports that Indian pilots had used new technology and unconventional tactics very effectively against aging U.S. fighters in recent air exercises.[3]

Air Force leaders felt strongly that both developments reflected a more generalized erosion in U.S. air capabilities. The top-of-the-line F-15C air-superiority fighter had been designed in the 1960s, and by the turn of the century was so old that it flew training missions on flight restriction because of age-related metal fatigue. One Air Force general had the unsettling experience of losing all his cockpit instrumentation while flying over northern Iraq because the insulation on wiring had rotted away, resulting in a short circuit between exposed wires. (He later discovered he was flying the same F-15 he had first operated as a junior officer in the 1970s.)[4]

From the Air Force's perspective, such stories underscored the urgency of replacing Cold War tactical aircraft with a new generation of stealthy fighters. The problem wasn't just that existing fighters had grown decrepit with age, but also the fact that since they had been designed, there had been huge advances in technology that couldn't be fully incorporated into legacy airframes. The Indian air force had proved that new sensors and data links could be installed in old planes, but there was no way those planes could assimilate the low-observable features that would make them nearly invisible to radar. That required fundamentally different airframes.

Senior policymakers participating in the quadrennial review didn't ignore these concerns, but they were more sanguine about the durability of U.S. air dominance than Air Force representatives were. They favored buying thousands of stealthy F-35 Joint Strike Fighters for future use by three services, rather than continuing production of the Air Force's F-22 "Raptor" replacement for the venerable F-15. However, the F-35 was a single-engine airframe conceived mainly as a tactical bomber rather than an air superiority plane. It lacked the thrust, maneuverability, and fuel-efficient speed of the F-22.[5]

The Air Force argued strenuously that it required a minimum of 381 F-22s to equip each of ten expeditionary air wings with a squadron of 24 Raptors (381 aircraft are needed to sustain 240 combat-coded planes due to training, maintenance, and other backup requirements). It offered to give up 600 Joint Strike Fighters—about a third of its planned buy—to secure the 200 more Raptors needed to reach that goal. But policymakers rejected that offer, because a cut in the Air Force buy of F-35s would increase the average cost of F-35s for the Navy and Marine Corps. In effect, the Air Force was compelled to terminate its highest-priority aircraft modernization program at about half of the desired goal in order to support the modernization efforts of other services.

This debate was widely depicted in the media as an arcane exchange between contending bureaucracies, but for the Air Force it was about life and death. Service leaders didn't believe they could sustain global air dominance to midcentury without an adequate number of F-22s. In the absence of air dominance, other facets of air power wouldn't matter much, because the service couldn't ensure the survival of its fleet in combat. The whole point of buying the F-22 was to sweep the sky of enemy fighters during the early days of a future war and then work in tandem with other joint assets to suppress ground defenses. Once unfettered command of the air was achieved, the joint force could pursue additional tactical objectives. But without first asserting air dominance, it wasn't clear further goals would be attainable.

For the senior policymakers around Rumsfeld, other warfighting issues were more urgent. They were determined to fashion a postindustrial military posture responsive to the full range of emerging threats the nation faced, rather than overinvesting in conventional warfare. They called their approach "capability-based" planning, and it tended to focus investment priorities in areas where the United States didn't already have a decisive lead, such as intelligence-gathering capabilities. In their view, it was more important to bolster global reconnaissance of elusive adversaries and enhance collaborative warfighting skills than to pour money into heavy armor, sea power, and air power where the nation already had a substantial edge over prospective adversaries.[6]

The Air Force tried hard in the run-up to the quadrennial review and during deliberations to fashion a future posture responsive to the concerns of senior policymakers. It proposed a "beacon force" of future combat systems that would cut fighter inventories from 2,400 to 1,800 airframes while bolstering reconnaissance capabilities. It recast its core competencies around three overarching missions—global strike, global mobility, and global awareness—that highlighted the relevance of service competencies to joint needs. It invested heavily in information networks and space. But it couldn't convince Rumsfeld's team that air dominance was at risk, and it made little headway in presenting the case for buying any kind of manned aircraft other than the tri-service F-35.

A case in point was the E-10 surveillance aircraft, conceived by former Air Force chief of staff General John Jumper as a multimission replacement for the E-3 Airborne Warning and Control System (AWACS), E-8 Joint Surveillance and Target Attack Radar System (JSTARS), and RC-135 Rivet Joint eavesdropping plane. During Jumper's tenure—which overlapped the early months of the quadrennial review—the E-10 was second only to the F-22 as an Air Force modernization priority, because electronic surveillance missions were becoming more important to the joint force at the same time that so-called "low-density/high-demand" assets for conducting them were growing old. The basic idea behind the E-10 concept was that a common airframe would be procured in three variants for performing future airspace surveillance, ground surveillance, and eavesdropping missions.[7]

However, OSD policymakers, led by Dr. Stephen Cambone, the under secretary of defense for intelligence, consistently opposed the E-10 program, arguing that surveillance missions in the future should migrate from manned aircraft to unmanned aerial vehicles and spacecraft. Cambone viewed the E-10 concept as an outmoded approach to surveillance that failed to reflect changes in mission requirements and the potential of new technology. Air Force leaders didn't totally dismiss such thinking—in fact, they were spending considerable sums on developing unmanned aerial vehicles and next-generation spacecraft for conducting surveillance—but they didn't understand how mission needs could be accomplished unless manned aircraft were part of the mix. In the end, the E-10 program was scaled back to a single test aircraft, with no prospect of ever making the transition to production.

In fact, by the time quadrennial review deliberations wrapped up in late 2005, virtually every manned aircraft the service had in development or production, other than the Joint Strike Fighter, looked destined for termination. In addition to killing E-10, policymakers capped production of the F-22 fighter at 183 airframes (less than half of the stated requirement) and directed termination of both the C-17 and C-130 airlifters. The service was authorized to proceed with plans for a competition to begin replacing Eisenhower-era aerial refueling tankers, but that effort was so awash in controversy that it wasn't clear when a contract would actually be awarded.[8]

Bad as this outcome was for modernization of the air fleet, Air Force leaders breathed a sigh of relief when the process was over because the prospect of even worse results had loomed throughout the discussions. One possibility was that F-22 production would be ended immediately, rather than stretching into the next decade. Another was that development of the Air Force variant of F-35—over 70 percent of the entire joint production run—would be terminated, and the Air Force would then be forced to acquire the less suitable naval variant.[9] It is a measure of how low Air Force expectations had fallen going into the process that service leaders exited the quadrennial review convinced they had averted a disaster.

In reality, they had been forced to embrace a modernization plan that guaranteed further erosion of U.S. air power in the years ahead. Not only would the service not receive a sufficient number of air-superiority fighters to sustain future combat rotations, but it would prematurely exit airlift programs vital to other parts of the joint force and lack a clear path forward for preserving critical surveillance capabilities. The service had suffered bigger cuts in the 1990s, but given further aging of the fleet in subsequent years, the damage imposed by the 2005 Quadrennial Defense Review was arguably worse.[10]

Management Mistakes Erode Space Power

The strategic planning guidance generated by senior policymakers after the quadrennial review was completed directed the Air Force to emphasize satellites and unmanned aerial vehicles over manned aircraft in its development of future combat systems. It also directed all of the services to stress user needs over platform types in determining the best approach to meeting future reconnaissance requirements—guidance that was interpreted within the Air Force as further pressure to abandon manned aircraft in acquiring next-generation surveillance systems. Since OSD's issuance of strategic planning guidance is an early step in the annual budget cycle designed to shape service requests, the implication of such language was that Rumsfeld and his advisers intended to use the budget process to enforce the priorities established in the quadrennial review.

By the time the guidance was issued in early 2006, however, there were numerous signs that proposed alternatives to manned aircraft in reconnaissance and strike missions wouldn't be delivering big gains in capability anytime soon. In the case of unmanned aerial vehicles, their much-touted persistence in surveillance missions had not enabled warfighters to find key al-Qaeda operatives such as Osama bin Laden and Ayman al-Zawahiri, while plans to develop an unmanned vehicle for executing other types of combat missions were still in flux. Most observers expected unmanned systems such as the high-altitude, long-endurance Global Hawk aircraft eventually to make a big contribution to success on the battlefield, but there wasn't much evidence they could take the place of manned airframes in the most demanding missions, such as conducting surveillance in contested airspace.

Space systems were turning out to be an even bigger disappointment, due mainly to a series of management missteps during the 1990s that had left plans for next-generation reconnaissance and communications constellations in disarray. When Secretary Rumsfeld returned to the Pentagon in 2001 after a twenty-five-year absence, he had just completed service as chairman of a presidential commission reviewing national security space programs.[11] That experience convinced him that orbital systems were a vital but underutilized feature of the nation's defense posture—a feature that should figure prominently in plans for military transformation. He therefore set about reforming the way in which space systems were acquired and operated, with an eye toward using them more extensively in every facet of military operations.

Among other things, Rumsfeld designated the Air Force as executive agent for the management of military satellites, launch systems, and ground infrastructure (which included networks for processing and disseminating the output of orbital sensors). This step took the Air Force's traditional role in operating military space systems to a new level, putting it in charge of almost every orbital constellation the department was buying. Some outsiders complained that the fighter pilots who dominated Air Force leadership had never given space sufficient priority in their budgets or warfighting plans. But no other service possessed the depth of experience or technical talent to serve as executive agent for space, and Rumsfeld was loath to establish a new defense agency for such a specialized purpose. So the Air Force got the job.

Unfortunately, most of the key decisions concerning next-generation spacecraft had been made in the 1990s, and as Rumsfeld's tenure progressed it became increasingly clear they had been made badly. Every satellite program the Defense Department was funding faced budget shortfalls, schedule slippage, and technical problems. In an effort to reconcile reduced defense spending with modernization requirements, the Clinton administration had made a series of optimistic assumptions about national-security space that one by one were turning out to be wrong. Since these assumptions had driven the way in which satellite development efforts were structured, the Bush administration inherited a collection of severely impaired programs.[12]

First of all, the Clinton administration had assumed there would be robust commercial demand for space services during the first decade of the new millennium, which the Pentagon could leverage to achieve economies of scale in its own space efforts. That assumption melted down when the telecommunications boom of the late nineties went bust. Second, it assumed that commercial product specifications could be substituted for military specifications in designing next-generation spacecraft, an idea that led to endless confusion among contractors. Third, it assumed that more of the responsibility for managing spacecraft development programs could be vested in private industry rather than the government, a policy that resulted in the government losing much of its technical expertise for overseeing modernization. Finally, it assumed that a wider range of military users should have access to the services provided by satellites, which had the effect of greatly increasing the performance requirements and cost of those satellites.[13]

The cumulative impact of these misguided ideas on the space sector proved to be devastating. For example, the space-based infrared system conceived in 1994 to replace Cold War missile warning satellites ended up with eighteen "key performance parameters," which the Defense Science Board later determined was four times greater than the optimum number. The program eventually fell years behind schedule—so much so that policymakers began to worry the nation might lose its capacity to detect hostile missile launches by around 2015. An ambitious architecture to replace aging photo-reconnaissance satellites went billions of dollars over budget before Rumsfeld's advisers decided parts of the program were unexecutable as originally conceived. Similar problems arose on future communications and weather satellites.

It took some time for senior policymakers to grasp how serious were the problems in space. Rumsfeld's team actually made those problems worse at the beginning of his tenure by initiating new programs to transform space-based reconnaissance and communications, overburdening an already strained sector. But by the time Rumsfeld presided over his second quadrennial review in 2005, it should have been readily apparent to everyone in the Pentagon that national-security space was in deep trouble. Key development programs were failing to progress as planned, and congressional committees were refusing to fund new space initiatives at requested levels of expenditure until existing programs showed signs of improvement.

Against this backdrop, it is difficult to understand why proponents of transformation around Secretary Rumsfeld continued to push so hard for space-based alternatives to manned aircraft in missions such as the tracking of mobile ground targets. While there were sound, physics-based reasons for relying on satellites in building a global communications network, monitoring weather patterns, and providing navigation information to warfighters, the case for space-based reconnaissance was actually weakening. Not only were adversaries becoming more elusive—requiring closer, more continuous scrutiny of likely sanctuaries—but those sanctuaries tended to be located in places where there was little threat to U.S. surveillance planes. Satellite reconnaissance was still necessary for countries with well-defended airspace such as China, but in the places where America's military was most active, user needs dictated reliance on nearby aircraft rather than orbital sensors hundreds of miles away.

Nonetheless, senior policymakers continued to stress the importance of space systems in their investment plans, despite all the problems with next-generation spacecraft and the shift in operational needs. The Air Force thus confronted two major challenges in its modernization plans that together threatened the service's capacity to support the joint force in future warfare. On the one hand, its plan to replace aging aircraft was underfunded and failed to address emerging shortfalls in capability for global mobility, strike, and awareness. On the other, its program to modernize Cold War space systems had gone awry, raising doubts about whether the service could replace key satellites before they ceased to provide vital services to the nation's warfighters. The 2005 quadrennial review did little to resolve the first problem, and failed even to acknowledge the second.

Threat Assessments Sow Uncertainty

The difficulties Air Force leaders face in framing a coherent, affordable modernization strategy are traceable largely to the way in which threats have changed since the end of the Cold War. Prior to the collapse of communism, the entire history of the service had been consumed in two great struggles, one to defeat fascism and the other to contain communism. The posture and culture of the service were, therefore, oriented to coping with conventional military threats originating in other industrialized nations. The unconventional challenges that came to dominate policymaker concerns in the new millennium had existed in the past, but the Air Force had always treated them as a "lesser included case" rather than the primary threat.

By the time of the 2005 quadrennial review, this view of the world was beginning to look outmoded. Aside from the fact that no peer competitor for the U.S. military seemed likely to arise for decades to come, the nation had managed to suffer significant setbacks at the hands of unconventional enemies about once a decade since the middle of the twentieth century. Defeat in Vietnam in the 1970s was followed by an ignominious retreat from Lebanon in the '80s, a farcical performance in Somalia in the '90s, and uneven counterinsurgency efforts in Southwest Asia after 9/11. But despite repeated warnings from intelligence analysts and outside experts that "asymmetric" (unconventional) threats had become the predominant challenge to U.S. influence around the globe, the Air Force and other services were slow to adjust to new realities.

The ambivalent response of service leaders to new threats was readily apparent during the early stages of the quadrennial review.

Senior policymakers produced a matrix of future military challenges that downgraded the priority of traditional, conventional threats while highlighting the danger posed by irregular forces, nuclear weapons proliferation, and disruptive technology breakthroughs. Air Force leaders acknowledged in principle that all of these asymmetric challenges (and others) were growing, but argued that the low apparent danger posed by conventional threats was an illusion—the main reason adversaries were taking the asymmetric route was that the United States so thoroughly dominated the means for waging conventional warfare. If the nation failed to maintain its superiority in air power and other forms of conventional capability, they said, enemies would have an incentive to invest more heavily in those areas.

In fact, the Air Force argued strongly that such a shift was already in progress, pointing to the spread of increasingly capable tactical aircraft, integrated air defenses, and long-range cruise missiles in countries such as China, India, and Iran. A series of classified warfighting scenarios conducted as part of the quadrennial review tended to confirm the Air Force's case. For example, a scenario involving China found that a combination of agile fighters and networked ground defenses might deny aging U.S. aircraft access to Chinese airspace in a future war, while sophisticated sea mines, ultraquiet diesel-electric subs, and anti-ship cruise missiles would keep U.S. naval forces far from Chinese shores. China's investment in mobile, deceptively based ballistic missiles that could hit the United States and regional Asian targets would also present Washington with powerful disincentives to waging war in the western Pacific. Beyond that, the Chinese were said to be experimenting with ways of degrading U.S. space systems and disrupting military information networks.

Senior policymakers acknowledged the importance of military trends in China and other Asian nations in strategic planning and subsequently directed the Air Force and Navy to deploy more of their warfighting assets permanently in the western Pacific. But their assessment of future challenges placed more emphasis on nontraditional threats for which the Air Force had few ready responses. First of all, they were extremely concerned that terrorists or other extreme actors would secure access to weapons of mass destruction—nuclear, chemical, or biological. Second, they were worried that the United States lacked effective counters to the kinds of irregular warfare being waged by insurgents in Iraq and Afghanistan. Third, they were convinced that if the United States failed to fully leverage new technologies emerging from the information revolution, its military power might be circumvented or surpassed by more forward-looking nations.

None of these concerns matched up very well with the traditional competencies of the Air Force. Keeping weapons of mass destruction out of the hands of terrorists was mainly about improving U.S. intelligence capabilities, but the airborne and orbital reconnaissance systems in which the Air Force specialized were better suited to tracking conventional military forces than elusive adversaries. The skills for waging effective counterinsurgency warfare were embedded mainly in the ground forces. And while the Air Force had a long record of leveraging advanced aerospace technologies, it was not as adept at exploiting the networking technologies that policymakers thought were most important in the current era. So while there was little question that the Air Force could make important contributions in all of the areas of greatest concern to senior policymakers, there was also a decided mismatch between what worried them and what preoccupied the leadership of the service.

The Air Force thus ended up with a tiered, or compartmentalized, view of emerging threats that succeeded in accommodating service, joint, and national concerns only by generating a very extensive array of future operational requirements. At the service level, concern was focused most frequently on coping with perceived challenges to U.S. air and space power, particularly the spread of new air-to-air and surface-to-air systems that might negate U.S. tactical aircraft. At the joint level, concern was focused on the various anti-access strategies of prospective adversaries that might impede the Air Force's capacity to support the joint force in overseas operations. At the national level, concern was focused on the emergence of unconventional enemies whose defeat would require more attention to human intelligence, homeland defense, special operations, and a range of other previously neglected activities.

Diverse Threats Drive Demanding Requirements

During the Cold War, virtually all of the Air Force's operational requirements were outgrowths of the military threat posed by the Soviet Union. Although the service never really came up with a satisfactory answer to the challenge posed by thousands of Soviet nuclear warheads—nuclear deterrence was essentially a theoretical construct rather than a proven path to security—there was never any doubt that the Russian threat was the threat that mattered. Military planners were so absorbed by that danger that all other requirements were subsumed in preparations for war with the Eastern Bloc.

The situation today is completely different. A single, stark challenge to the survival of democracy has been replaced by a diverse array of nascent threats, some of which have hardened into real dangers, and others of which are largely conjectural. Even in cases where the danger is well-defined, as with al-Qaeda, there is little agreement about how durable the threat will be, or what kind of strategy can best defeat it. Not surprisingly, this confusing strategic landscape has produced an unwieldy, even contradictory, compendium of future operational requirements for the Air Force.[14] The most important ones—those that have translated into major investment programs—can be separated into five categories: sustaining aerospace superiority; maintaining information dominance; enhancing global awareness; providing global mobility; and expanding global strike capabilities.

Aerospace Superiority. The purpose of the series of operational requirements assigned highest priority by Air Force leaders is to ensure that the service can continue to exercise unfettered dominance in global airspace and in orbit. In the case of airspace, that means acquiring tactical aircraft of sufficient quantity and quality to defeat any air-to-air and surface-to-air challenges likely to arise between now and midcentury. In addition to being lethal and survivable under the most trying circumstances, these aircraft must have the connectivity and sensing capacity to suppress whatever networks or other novel technologies adversaries might field to deny access to their airspace. Furthermore, the next generation of tactical aircraft must be able to escort and protect less agile aircraft crossing hostile airspace so that they can accomplish reconnaissance, strike, and logistics missions in support of the entire joint force. The service is investing extensively in munitions, sensors, and communications systems relevant to preserving air dominance, but the main thrust of its modernization in this mission area is the replacement of Cold War fighters with a new generation of stealthy tactical aircraft.

Outside the earth's atmosphere, sustaining superiority means successfully orbiting a new generation of spacecraft to replace existing surveillance, communications, navigation, and weather satellites. It also means developing ground networks capable of merging, manipulating, and disseminating the output of these orbital assets for the broadest range of friendly users in forms that are immediately useful and relevant. A related requirement receiving increased attention is to negate whatever efforts countries such as China may mount to degrade the space-based assets of the United States, whether they be direct attacks on satellites in orbit, jamming of signals, or sabotage of ground stations. Policymakers have become increasingly concerned in recent years that as U.S. forces become more dependent on information generated by or transmitted through space systems, the value to enemies of disrupting or destroying those systems increases correspondingly.

Information Dominance. Information dominance is the cluster of future operational requirements that concern control of the electromagnetic spectrum and cyberspace.[15] A key feature of military transformation as currently interpreted is the management of information flows relevant to warfighters, so that friendly forces always have access to the most timely and useful knowledge while adversaries are denied similar insight. In order to create such an asymmetry on the battlefield, U.S. forces must be able to ensure the survival and integrity of their critical networks under the most demanding circumstances. They must also be able to disrupt, degrade, or destroy the networks of enemies. The Air Force has been assigned a leading role in the joint community for such activities.

In practice, the future operational requirements for information dominance break down into a series of arcane skills in which the Air Force and other services must be proficient. In the area of electronic warfare, the Air Force must be able to suppress enemy sensors, communications networks, and command centers despite the efforts of adversaries to hide or harden them. Depending on the nature of the targets and the warfighting assets available, this might be achieved through jamming, deception, or outright destruction. In the related area of information warfare, the Air Force must be able to invade, impede, or disable enemy computers using a range of kinetic and nonkinetic effects including electromagnetic pulse and the planting of corrupted information. In the area of information assurance, the Air Force must be able to counter the aggressive moves of adversaries against U.S. networks, including hacking, sabotage, and other exotic methods. Although information dominance is still in its infancy as a focus of warfighting plans, the operational requirements to achieve it are expected to be diverse and demanding.

Global Awareness. Global awareness comprises the cluster of missions and activities associated with what the military calls intelligence, surveillance, and reconnaissance (ISR). All of the services engage in the collection and analysis of information relevant to military operations, but the Air Force is the dominant provider of such information to the joint force and national agencies by virtue of its lead role in space and its ownership of the most capable airborne reconnaissance systems. The Defense Department currently operates eight different satellite constellations for the collection of imagery, signals intelligence, missile warning indications, and weather data; additional constellations exist to provide secure worldwide transmission of the intelligence collected by orbital and airborne sensors. The Air Force plays a central role in the operation of these assets, as it does in the design and management of six next-generation ISR constellations currently in development. It also operates a dozen specialized types of ISR aircraft—manned and unmanned—such as the E-3 AWACS, E-8 JSTARS, RC-135 Rivet Joint, RQ-1 Predator, and RQ-4 Global Hawk.[16]

Air Force leaders view global awareness as one of their service's core competencies. However, the range of operational requirements associated with meeting the future ISR needs of the joint force and national agencies is so imposing that the service could easily expend its entire modernization budget on global awareness without achieving all of the desired capabilities.

Not only have threats shifted in a way that requires a complete redesign of the global intelligence-gathering and reconnaissance system, but senior policymakers have repeatedly complained that the network for processing and disseminating critical intelligence is gravely dysfunctional. To put it bluntly, current ISR systems cannot find, fix, or track the adversaries of greatest interest with any degree of consistency, and, if they could, it is not clear that the information would reach warfighters in a timely fashion. So although the service has made good progress in some areas, such as compressing the kill cycle of time-sensitive targets, it faces a daunting challenge in developing new approaches to ISR and integrating the network for exploiting militarily relevant information.

Global Mobility. Compared with the future operational requirements for global awareness, the requirements for global mobility are relatively simple and straightforward. The Air Force operates a fleet of nearly 300 intertheater cargo planes and over 500 intratheater cargo planes to provide airlift and logistics to the joint force. It also owns about 600 aerial refueling tankers essential to extending the range and endurance of other military aircraft. Without these mobility assets, it would be nearly impossible for the United States to project its power rapidly overseas, and whole sectors of the military establishment would be rendered useless. For example, the Army is designing its future combat systems around the presumed availability of C-17 transports for rapid force insertion, and naval aviation has relied heavily on Air Force tankers to sustain air operations in the Balkans, Afghanistan, and Iraq.[17]

The most immediate need in the global mobility arena is to determine what amount of airlift is required through midcentury, because the Bush administration is planning to close both major production lines for military cargo planes—those for the C-17 jet in California and the C-130 turboprop in Georgia. Some analysts believe the current fleet isn't capable of meeting future requirements, especially given depressed mission-capable rates for the legacy C-5 jet transport and the advanced age of many earlier-model C-130s. Trends in the civil air fleet are likely to make it a less reliable backup to military airlift in the future.[18] The other pressing near-term requirement is to commence modernization of the tanker fleet, about 90 percent of which was built during the Eisenhower and Kennedy administrations. Although the tanker fleet is still in reasonably good shape despite an average airframe age of over forty years, it will probably take decades to replace all the planes. Modernization must begin soon if the Air Force is to avoid flying sixty-year-old tankers one day. Beyond these issues, the Air Force needs to determine how it will reorganize its airlift and refueling fleets within the joint logistics system to achieve more efficient use of scarce assets.

Global Strike. Global strike is the mission area involving all uses of disabling force against enemies—kinetic and nonkinetic, lethal and nonlethal. During the Cold War, Air Force strike capabilities were concentrated mainly in missile silos and heavy bombers. Once the Soviet Union collapsed, many strike missions migrated to tactical aircraft. The F-35 Joint Strike Fighter was conceived to, among other things, provide the Air Force with a stealthy successor to the F-16 that could deliver precision munitions against a wide array of hardened, dispersed, or otherwise demanding targets. But even before the F-35 entered production, the threat had begun evolving in ways that made new approaches to global strike necessary. Not only were emerging threats harder to localize and track, but political considerations sometimes dictated that they be addressed using minimally destructive methods.

The most urgent unmet strike requirement identified by the 2005 quadrennial review was the need to address time-sensitive targets anywhere in the world within a few minutes. The Air Force had no ready response to this requirement because all of the tools in its inventory were either too slow or too gross in their effects. It now has been charged with finding a more cost-effective answer than equipping long-range ballistic missiles with conventional warheads. A broader, longer-term requirement is to replace aging heavy bombers with a more flexible and persistent airframe, possibly one that is unmanned. Although the service is expected to operate hundreds of strike-capable fighters for the foreseeable future, these planes lack the range, payload, and endurance necessary to address some targets. More generally, the Air Force needs to think through how newly available technologies, such as directed energy, cyberwarfare tools, and nonlethal weapons should be integrated into the existing arsenal of more traditional munitions. Some of these new technologies could provide unique opportunities for tailoring effects, but that depends on whether the necessary target reconnaissance and concepts of operation are available to warfighters.[19]

A Handful of Programs Will Determine the Fate of Air Power

The Air Force manages scores of technology development programs, either to satisfy its own organic needs or to meet the broader, security-related requirements of the joint force and national agencies. Some of these programs, such as the multibillion-dollar effort to enhance orbital eavesdropping capabilities, are not discussed in public and cannot be readily analyzed by outsiders. However, most of the programs essential to preserving the sinews of air and space dominance are well-known. The reasons they are essential can best be understood by relating each effort to the five clusters of requirements cited above.

Aerospace Superiority. The Air Force believes it cannot sustain global air dominance to midcentury without a sufficient number of stealthy F-22 Raptor fighters. The F-22 is a twin-engine replacement for the top-of-the-line F-15C that will provide unprecedented agility, survivability, and fuel-efficient speed. The service defines sufficiency as at least 381 F-22s, the number needed to equip each of ten expeditionary air wings with a squadron of 24 Raptors (including backup, test, and attrition aircraft). Under pressure from the Office of the Secretary of Defense, the Air Force agreed to cut its buy of F-22s to

183 airframes, and to consider operating squadrons of 18 rather than 24 planes. However, nobody in the service's senior leadership believes that the reduced production run and squadron size are suitable for sustaining combat rotations in future conflicts. Moreover, it makes little sense to fund a costly development program through five administrations and then slash production just as the program is coming to fruition. Therefore, the plan to terminate production prematurely is likely to be revisited in the next administration.

The Air Force currently plans to make a much larger investment in its version of the tri-service F-35 Joint Strike Fighter. If the program is implemented as presently planned, the service will buy nearly 1,800 conventional-takeoff-and-landing F-35s. However, Air Force leaders would gladly trade a third of their F-35 buy to meet their goal of 381 F-22s, recognizing that it is better to have a smaller, balanced fleet of tactical aircraft than a larger, unbalanced one. The single-engine F-35 will be just as stealthy as an F-22, but will lack the speed and agility to cope with emerging threats. Indeed, the original concept of operations envisioned F-22s and F-35s operating in tandem, an approach that can't work if there are too few Raptors to protect all of the fielded F-35s. The service would prefer to buy 1,100 F-35s and about twice the number of F-22s currently programmed. But although this tradeoff would seem to satisfy future requirements while saving money, it complicates purchase of Joint Strike Fighters by the sea services (due to diminished economies of scale), while requiring more money up front to sustain F-22 production as F-35 output is also ramping up.

In terms of preserving space superiority, the Air Force is currently leading Defense Department efforts to modernize every major constellation of spacecraft—communications, navigation, missile warning, and so on—at a cost of about $10 billion annually, not counting classified programs. The individual spacecraft programs are discussed later in this section, but two other considerations related to preserving space dominance merit mention here. First, the service needs to secure its space-launch capabilities through continued support of the evolved expendable launch vehicle, a program that ensures access to space by funding two separate families of rockets relying on different designs and technology. Second, the service needs to continue developing technologies for the defense of U.S. space assets against direct attack, jamming, or intrusion. Space systems provide U.S. forces with unique warfighting leverage, but there is evidence that some potential enemies intend to disrupt or destroy U.S. satellite operations in future conflicts, and those moves must be countered.[20]

Information Dominance. The Air Force is the leading service in developing technology for control of the electromagnetic spectrum and cyberspace in future conflicts. For example, a series of Air Force experiments codenamed Project Suter have explored how the joint force could invade enemy communications networks and computers to impair command functions. The service has also developed a range of nontraditional munitions for shutting down electrical and communications grids without causing gross physical damage or human suffering. These efforts, largely secret, are essential to establishing information dominance against future adversaries who will have access to many of the same cutting-edge technologies as U.S. forces.

However, despite considerable progress in exploring the requirements for information dominance, the Air Force's plan to modernize its key electronic attack and information-warfare assets is in disarray. Not only has the E-10 electronic aircraft, conceived (among other things) to replace existing eavesdropping planes, been effectively terminated, but the service has also canceled its plan to provide standoff jamming of enemy sensors and communications links using modified B-52 bombers. The latter move was overdue, because even if the program had not encountered cost growth, penetrating aircraft require escort jamming rather than standoff protection for electronic warfare missions. But it is not clear what alternative the service will pursue, given uncertainties about the survivability of unmanned aerial vehicles in hostile airspace and the dearth of funding for modifying manned aircraft. Termination of the E-10 is a much harder pill for service leaders to swallow, because alternative approaches to satisfying future tactical eavesdropping and surveillance needs are unattractive, and maybe even unexecutable. In particular, the Air Force needs to identify a plan for replacing its critically important

RC-135 Rivet Joint signals intelligence aircraft, which despite continuous improvement are unlikely to satisfy joint information-warfare needs after 2020.[21]

Beyond the various arcane programs associated with electronic attack and cyberwarfare, information dominance in the future will depend in large measure on the creation of joint networks that offer sufficient capacity, access, and resilience to support the dynamic needs of a worldwide force. Among the welter of networking initiatives that the Air Force currently funds, two stand out as deserving the highest priority: the fielding of a joint tactical radio system that can replace diverse legacy radios with a software-programmable radio affording unprecedented interoperability; and the development of a transformational communications architecture that can replace existing communications satellites with a high-capacity, dynamically routed "Internet-in-the sky." It may be possible to evolve most of the technology for the latter capability out of an existing program to replace the Milstar satellite constellation. However, if either the joint tactical radio system or the transformational communications architecture falters, the promise of a netcentric Air Force will be compromised for the foreseeable future.[22]

Global Awareness. The dividing line between information dominance and global awareness is blurred at best, because information dominance begins with having good information. Several of the intelligence, surveillance, and reconnaissance programs most important to meeting global awareness requirements also play pivotal roles in information dominance. That is especially true with regard to manned aircraft, because the ill-fated E-10 electronic aircraft was supposed to provide a successor not only to Rivet Joint, but also to the E-3 AWACS and E-8 JSTARS surveillance planes. The disappearance of E-10 from the Air Force modernization plan thus creates a gap in future global awareness capabilities similar to its negative impact in the information-warfare arena. Without E-10, the Air Force does not have a clear path forward for sustaining the aerial surveillance and tracking role of AWACS or the ground surveillance and tracking role of JSTARS. In the near-term, legacy airframes will have to be repaired and upgraded to continue satisfying joint needs, but over the longer run there will have to be a new multimission surveillance aircraft similar to E-10. The Air Force is exploring options for meeting its future requirements and those of other services in a common airframe.

Unmanned aerial vehicles are likely to meet a growing range of global awareness needs in the future. The two most important unmanned aerial vehicle programs the Air Force currently funds are the RQ-1 Predator and the RQ-4 Global Hawk, both of which have demonstrated a capacity to provide persistence superior to that of any manned aircraft, and precision superior to that of reconnaissance satellites (spacecraft in geostationary orbit are 22,000 miles from objects on the earth's surface, while those in lower orbits move at several miles per second relative to the surface—thus lacking persistence). The Global Hawk vehicle in particular has proved to be an extremely versatile, long-endurance system, simultaneously collecting imagery, signals intelligence, and other types of intelligence during sorties lasting several times the length of a typical manned aircraft flight.[23] The ability to field a sufficient number of Predators and Global Hawks with the requisite sensor payloads and connectivity appears indispensable in satisfying emerging global awareness needs.

Space systems will continue to play a central part in global awareness, providing a unique vantage point from which sensors can penetrate areas otherwise closed to U.S. collection assets. While it is not feasible to discuss the various reconnaissance satellites that the Air Force is developing or operating in concert with the National Reconnaissance Office, two other spacecraft types look likely to make major contributions to global awareness for decades to come. First, the space-based infrared system replacing Cold War missile warning satellites will greatly increase the quantity and quality of intelligence available to strategic and tactical users in the infrared portion of the spectrum; coupled with a ground network already in operation for fusing and rapidly disseminating information from multiple sources, the new constellation will support nuclear deterrence, missile defense, tactical military operations, and intelligence community needs. Second, space radar has the potential to provide a leap in reconnaissance capabilities comparable to that which global positioning provided for navigation, enabling continuous tracking and imagery of moving targets anywhere on the earth's surface.[24]

Global Mobility. The future capacity of U.S. combat forces to deploy rapidly will be shaped by many factors, including the pre-positioning of equipment in likely theaters of operation, the availability of sealift, and the success of the Army in fielding lighter brigade combat teams. For the Air Force, though, the future of mobility comes down largely to the fate of three programs: the C-17 strategic airlifter, the C-130J tactical airlifter, and the proposed successor to the KC-135 tanker. At present, the service plans to terminate production of both the C-17 and C-130J in the near future, while beginning the long-delayed recapitalization of its Cold War tanker fleet. However, the decision to terminate airlift programs was grounded in a mobility requirements study that did not project airlift needs beyond 2012. Because lift requirements could grow considerably in later years, Army and Air Force leaders are skeptical about the wisdom of terminating production of the C-17 and C-130J. Unfortunately, funding is not currently available to continue airlift production while also beginning replacement of tankers.

The planned airlift fleet will consist of 111 giant C-5 cargo planes, 180 C-17s, and over 500 C-130s in a range of configurations. The jet-powered C-5s and C-17s were designed mainly for intertheater missions, while the propeller-driven C-130s were built mainly for intratheater missions. However, this distinction between "strategic" and "tactical" airlift is being blurred somewhat by the longer range and greater carrying capacity of the C-130 "J" variant. Although the venerable C-5 still has decades of service life remaining, changes in the threat, in operating concepts, and in airlift technology make the C-17 and C-130 more suitable for many missions. In addition, the C-5 has suffered from chronically low mission-capable rates, a problem the Air Force hopes to correct by installing new engines and electronics on the planes. When the demands of the global war on terror are combined with the advanced age of many C-130s in the field today, it is hard to see the wisdom of terminating either active airlift line. Not only is the C-17 essential to the success of the Army's future combat plans, but the C-130 is the logical candidate to fill a gap in short-hop cargo-carrying capacity. The Air Force therefore must find the money to keep both the C-17 and C-130J production lines active, while also upgrading the C-5 fleet.[25]

All of this might be feasible within projected funding limits if the Air Force were not determined to begin replacing its fleet of Eisenhower- and Kennedy-era aerial refueling tankers. But once that burden is added to the budget, it is clear only additional money outside the current program will make it possible to meet all future mobility requirements. KC-135s represent about 90 percent of the Air Force's refueling fleet, and the oldest of them are of doubtful airworthiness. Because this fleet supports the logistics needs of all services, and other facets of warfighting could not be accomplished without it, Air Force leaders are unwilling to wait any longer on recapitalization. Assuming that the KC-135s are replaced at a rate of two dozen planes per year, it will take about twenty years to fully modernize the fleet. With the typical KC-135 already averaging forty-five years of age, there is a possibility that metal fatigue, corrosion, or other age-related problems will begin reducing aerial refueling capacity long before modernization is due to be completed.[26] So Air Force leaders are right to insist on an early start to recapitalization, despite the impact its cost will have on competing needs.

Global Strike. No part of the Air Force's arsenal has seen a greater reversal of fortune over the last generation than the heavy bomber fleet. The intercontinental strike capability that made the service first among equals in military councils during the early Cold War period has shrunk to a fraction of its former size, and all of the planes in the force are aging fast. The 2005 Quadrennial Defense Review set the goal of developing by the year 2018 a new land-based, long-range strike system capable of penetrating hostile airspace. Since the same document cited a need for lengthy persistence and larger payloads in strike systems, the new initiative may evolve into a next-generation bomber. Some observers have speculated that the future bomber could be unmanned, but that seems unlikely, given the projected survivability of unmanned vehicles that must penetrate and sustain operations in contested airspace. Whatever solution the service settles on, rescuing the bomber force from its current low ebb should be a high priority.[27]

In the near term, steps must be taken to upgrade the three heavy bombers already in the fleet, because these planes are likely to provide the backbone of long-range strike capabilities for decades to come. Whatever new strike system (if any) the service begins fielding in 2018 will only enter the force gradually, meaning that bombers in the force today must remain combat-ready until at least 2030. Congress has repeatedly resisted efforts to retire a portion of these existing bombers, and, given the likelihood of attrition in future conflicts, that stance is probably correct. It makes little sense, however, to retain aging bombers if steps are not taken to improve their targeting, connectivity, and self-protection capabilities. Therefore, additional money will be needed to renew the current bomber inventory even as the Air Force develops a more capable replacement.[28]

Due to budget constraints, competing needs, and changes in the threat, the Air Force is almost certain to buy fewer F-35 Joint Strike Fighters than the 1,800 it currently has programmed. But the service will need to acquire at least 1,100 F-35s so it can replace aging fighter-bombers and attack-aircraft in tactical strike roles. It will also need to continue developing next-generation communications networks and targeting sensors to ensure these planes can be used to maximum effect. One key issue that must be closely monitored as U.S. munitions become increasingly dependent on signals from the space-based global positioning system is whether planned constellations can withstand the efforts of adversaries to degrade them through jamming or direct attack. Orbiting a new generation of GPS III satellites is one of the most important steps military planners can take to ensure that future strike weapons operate as advertised.[29]

Preserving U.S. Air Power Will Require More Money

The preceding analysis has identified major gaps in Air Force modernization plans that could translate into a marked erosion of U.S. air power during the next two decades. In the area of aerospace superiority, the service needs to continue production of the F-22 fighter until all 381 planes required to sustain future combat rotations are acquired, without undercutting development of the F-35 Joint Strike Fighter destined for use by three different services. In the area of information dominance, the service needs to develop an escort jammer that can bolster the survivability of penetrating strike aircraft. In the area of global awareness, the service needs to fund a program similar to the canceled E-10 electronic aircraft that can provide a successor to AWACS, JSTARS, and the Rivet Joint eavesdropping plane. In the area of global mobility, the service needs to sustain production lines for existing airlift programs while commencing replacement of decrepit aerial refueling tankers. And in the area of global strike, it needs to begin development of a new, long-range bomber.

It is no coincidence that all of the big shortfalls in the modernization plan involve aircraft. After buying an average of 262 airframes per year during the 1970s and '80s, Air Force purchases plummeted to 60 per year in the '90s, and look likely to average only 84 per year in the current decade.[30] As a result, every category of airframe in the Air Force arsenal—fighters, bombers, transports, tankers, electronic aircraft—are exhibiting signs of advanced age. This pattern was so pronounced by the beginning of the new millennium that many observers assumed the Bush administration would greatly increase funding for aircraft modernization. But changing threats and intellectual fashions have conspired to prevent such an increase, and the stage is now set for a prolonged erosion in Air Force capabilities. To put it succinctly, spacecraft and communications networks have faced little difficulty in winning funding during the current decade, but manned aircraft have not gotten the money they needed.

Secretary Rumsfeld and his key advisers were right to question whether the joint force should modernize Cold War weapons platforms, given changes in the threat and the emergence of new technologies. But they have failed to advance a coherent alternative to service modernization agendas, and some of their program-specific initiatives to terminate high-priority programs like F-22 are fiscally and operationally irresponsible. Whatever the virtues of wireless networking and joint cooperation may be, the simple reality is that U.S. air power—arguably the single biggest advantage U.S. forces have on the battlefield—is declining. The only way to reverse this trend is to buy more planes, and to buy them fast before some unnoticed defect in aging tankers or transports compromises the capacity of the joint force to win wars.

Although the Air Force follows the practice of sister services in producing an annual compendium of unfunded priorities,[31] it has not generated a rigorous analysis of the full funding requirements necessary to sustain all facets of air power to midcentury. The reason it has not is that such an assessment would inevitably call into question the priorities of senior policymakers, while providing legislators with an agenda of program initiatives at odds with administration goals. But with barely two years left in office, the priorities of the Bush administration will soon be replaced anyway, so it is useful to understand what Air Force leaders truly think they would need to sustain core competencies in the future.

Discussions with various experts inside and outside the service suggest that the shortfall in Air Force investment accounts during the period 2008–13 is roughly $10 billion annually. About $3 billion per year would be needed to fund a more robust modernization effort in the air superiority area, although some of this increase could be recovered later if an additional buy of 200 F-22 fighters enabled the service to cut 600 F-35s out of its Joint Strike Fighter buy (cumulative costs would increase in the near term due to the different stages at which the programs now stand in the acquisition cycle). Another $3 billion, roughly, would be needed each year in the global mobility area to sustain existing airlift production lines, while still making an early start on tanker modernization. The remaining monies would be distributed across the information dominance, global awareness, and global strike areas to revitalize electronic warfare, airborne surveillance, and long-range bomber fleets.

Additional budget authority of $10 billion annually would amount to an 18 percent increase above Air Force funding for research, development, and procurement in 2006 (not counting supplemental appropriations and hidden accounts for classified intelligence activities). It would add 2–3 percent to the Defense Department's projected budgets through the end of the decade, which the administration currently sees stabilizing at about $450 billion per year (in 2006 constant dollars) after 2008.[32] While all the assumptions surrounding these calculations are likely to change, the added amount would not represent a big additional burden, especially when compared with the fiscal consequences of failing to prevail in future wars. The impact of additional investment outlays could be ameliorated if Congress allowed the Air Force to retire aircraft it says it no longer needs, shut down superfluous bases, reduce headcount in specialties not expected to experience high demand, and contract out for noncore services.

Of course, any military organization can assert the priority of its own needs, and claim minimal fiscal consequences to funding them once hypothetical savings are booked. At least one other military service—the Army—has been arguing for years that it should be receiving a bigger share of the defense budget at the expense of other military departments to better cover its own pressing needs. While the Army certainly does have pressing needs, especially given the burden it must bear for doing most of the fighting in Iraq, the merit of its demand for more of the military budget is undermined by the fact that so much of the Air Force's money—for airlift, for reconnaissance, for close air support—is already spent in support of Army missions. The reason no U.S. soldier has been killed by hostile military aircraft since 1953 has relatively little to do with how the Army spends its money, and a whole lot to do with where the Air Force has invested.

In the end, the debate surrounding funding of Air Force modernization comes down to a stark question about how little is enough. The pattern of aging across the Air Force's fleet of combat aircraft is undeniable, as is the fact that the nation has underinvested in military aircraft for a generation. The only reason such trends have been allowed to persist for so long is the absence of threats that could fully test U.S. air power. But just as asymmetric threats emerged in response to overwhelming U.S. conventional capabilities, so new threats will arise if that edge is allowed to erode. In the case of air power, the decay is now well advanced. If the focus of national security concerns shifts again, as it already has once in this decade, policymakers may find the global reach and global power they thought they had inherited from their Cold War predecessors increasingly a thing of the past.

4

Numbers and Capabilities: Building a Navy for the Twenty-First Century

Robert O. Work

Naval warfare—that is, fleet-on-fleet combat—is essentially about sinking another navy's ships. In competitions among naval powers, then, those that have bigger navies have an inherent advantage. In the eighteenth, nineteenth, and early twentieth centuries, a period marked by intense naval competition, the relative ranking of navies was often derived by comparing their overall fleet numbers, and particularly their number of "capital ships."[1]

After 1890, when the United States decided to compete against the world's top naval powers, the U.S. Navy became obsessed with metrics, such as its overall number of ships and aggregate fleet tonnage. In 1945, as World War II came to a close, the Navy's battle fleet numbered no less than 6,768 ships of all types, surpassing the British Royal Navy as the largest and most powerful naval force in the world in terms of tonnage, number of ships, and manpower.[2] It was, without doubt, "incomparably the greatest Navy in the world."[3]

If numbers tell the whole story, the U.S. fleet has been steadily diminishing in capability ever since. In the war's immediate aftermath, with no enemy fleet to fight, no forward bases to seize, and an emerging nuclear competition with the Soviet Union diverting most defense resources to the newly established U.S. Air Force, the Navy's battle fleet was gutted. By 1950, it had shrunk to just 634 ships, a staggering 90 percent reduction from its World War II high.[4]

The Korean War temporarily reversed this decline, although the numbers never again approached those of World War II. In the twenty-five years between 1954 and 1979—a period in which the Navy adjusted to account for the triple threat of high-speed jet aircraft, fast-attack submarines, and long-range missiles—the fleet averaged between 800 and 900 ships.[5] After the Vietnam War, as defense expenditures were once again cut, and as many modernized World War II–era ships reached the end of their service lives, the battle fleet began to shrink once more, reaching a post–World War II low of 521 ships in 1981.[6]

At this point, however, political leaders began to take heed of the alarm being raised over the possible loss of U.S. naval supremacy to a new challenger—the Soviet Navy.[7] Heartened by strong support from the administration and Congress, the Navy published a new maritime strategy that the famed naval historian Alfred Thayer Mahan would have instantly recognized and appreciated.[8] Its associated "600-ship Navy"—with force level goals of 100 nuclear attack submarines, 15 aircraft carrier battle groups, 4 battleship surface-action groups, and an amphibious fleet capable of lifting the assault echelons of a Marine amphibious force and amphibious brigade—was specifically designed to regain and maintain U.S. naval superiority over the Soviet Navy.[9]

With the abrupt implosion of the Soviet Union and its powerful navy in the early '90s the U.S. Navy once again faced the specter of a major demobilization. By 1995, its battle fleet had dropped below 400 ships for the first time since before World War II. Two years later—with the fleet at 365 ships and still shrinking—Navy leaders used the first congressionally mandated Quadrennial Defense Review to establish a floor for the post–Cold War fleet drawdown. They concluded that 300 ships was a level below which the fleet could not be allowed to fall, and they grudgingly accepted an ultimate target of some 302 ships.[10]

In truth, however, naval advocates both inside and outside the Navy found it difficult to accept a fleet that numbered only 300 ships, and they took every opportunity to call publicly for more. Indeed, after the second QDR, in 2001, endorsed a 307-ship Navy,[11] Admiral Vern Clark, then chief of naval operations, announced a new naval Global Concept of Operations with an associated battle fleet numbering 375 vessels—a plan that was roundly cheered by the Navy's rank and file, naval proponents, and the U.S. shipbuilding industry.[12]

However, with rising personnel expenses, escalating ship costs, and the unexpected costs associated with a newly declared global war on terror and its first two campaigns, operations Enduring Freedom and Iraqi Freedom, the Navy found it difficult to maintain even 300 ships. To free up money to help recapitalize the fleet, Admiral Clark reluctantly had to order the decommissioning of all remaining *Spruance*-class destroyers and the first five *Ticonderoga*-class guided-missile cruisers long before the ends of their thirty-five-year expected service lives.[13] Consequently, in 2003, the fleet fell right through the 300-ship floor set by the Navy six years earlier. As 2004 came to a close, the official count, known as the total ship battle force, stood at 288, and Department of Navy officials expected it to fall to about 280 before beginning to rebound.[14]

For those who equated combat capability with fleet numbers, the "incredible shrinking Navy" was becoming progressively weaker. Indeed, more than a few warned that the "300-ship Navy" was on the verge of losing its six-decade-old lead as the world's number one naval power, threatening America's standing as a global superpower.[15]

Losing Its Lead?

Certainly, at some point, the total number of ships in the battle fleet becomes operationally relevant, since a lack of overall numbers or a deficiency in specific types of ships or platforms will constrain a commander's options in developing plans and responses to contingencies. However, those who dwell solely on the number of ships in the fleet and who compare past and current numbers fail to take into account other metrics indicating that the contemporary 300-ship Navy is a force with combat power to spare.

For example, because of advances brought about in the 1990s by revolutions in guided weapons warfare and networking, along with the proliferation of the new Mk 41 shipboard vertical launch system

(VLS), fleet firepower dramatically increased.[16] In 1989, the 108 large surface combatants then in commission carried a total of 1,525 VLS cells and had an aggregate magazine capacity of 7,133 battle-force missiles (that is, long-range surface-to-air missiles, antisubmarine rockets, Harpoon anti-ship missiles, and Tomahawk land-attack missiles).[17] The 2004 surface-combatant fleet of seventy-one battle-force-capable combatants, despite having thirty-seven fewer ships, carried no less than 6,923 VLS cells and a fleet magazine capacity of 7,539 battle-force missiles. Similarly, the maximum theoretical daily strike capacity for the 1989 U.S. fleet of thirteen deployable carriers (with another in long-term overhaul) was 2,106 aimpoints. In 2004, because every "striker" on a carrier deck was capable of employing guided weapons, the comparative figure for eleven deployable carriers (with another in long-term overhaul) was more than 7,600 aimpoints.[18] In other words, today's 300-ship fleet boasts more aggregate striking power than the 1989 fleet nearly twice its size.

Of course, the Navy was not the only service that benefited from the guided weapons warfare revolution or increased joint-force planning and operations—all the services did, and none more so than the U.S. Air Force. One can now easily imagine a B-2 bomber armed with no less than eighty guided weapons penetrating a littoral ahead of an advancing naval battle force and methodically pulverizing an enemy's over-the-horizon targeting radars, coastal artillery and missile batteries, or ships at anchor—a point that often gets lost or minimized when focusing simply on the size of the fleet.

More importantly, although the U.S. total ship battle force is the smallest it has been in over seventy years, so, too, are the rest of the world's navies.[19] Indeed, as 2004 came to a close, only seven countries besides the United States operated war fleets that displaced more than 100,000 aggregate tons, and ten more operated fleets that displaced between 50,000 and 100,000 tons. Together, these seventeen navies accounted for 2.66 million tons.[20] In comparison, on December 31, 2004, the U.S. Navy operated a fleet of fighting warships with an aggregate displacement of 2.85 million tons. In terms of aggregate warship tonnage, then, the United States enjoyed a seventeen-navy standard.

Moreover, fourteen of the seventeen navies belonged to countries allied with or friendly to the United States, with a fifteenth, India, emerging as a new "strategic partner." Only two of the seventeen countries can reasonably be considered potential naval competitors: Russia and the People's Republic of China. The Russian Navy— assuming all of its ships are 100 percent operationally capable— comes in at 630,628 tons, while the Chinese People's Liberation Army Navy (PLAN) totals 263,064 tons. This means that the U.S. battle fleet out-displaces the combined fleets of its two biggest potential competitors by over three to one.[21]

As the foregoing numbers attest, then, despite being smaller than some past U.S. battle fleets, today's 300-ship Navy is likely the most powerful that has ever sailed the seas, and it is in no immediate danger of losing its place as the number one world naval force.

Coming to Terms with a 300-Ship Navy

By 2005, the combination of the battle fleet's increased combat power, the Navy's commanding lead among world naval powers, and continued budget pressures had undercut calls for a fleet much larger than 300 ships. In March 2005, Admiral Clark, the chief of naval operations, sent an interim thirty-year shipbuilding report to Congress that forecast a future fleet of somewhere between 260 and 325 ships, depending on the level of available resources, the pace of technological innovation, and the outcome of ongoing experiments in manning ships with multiple crews (which would allow a smaller fleet to maintain the same level of presence as a larger one).[22]

Admiral Clark knew that a shipbuilding plan that covered such a wide range of ships was likely to unsettle both Congress and the shipbuilding industry. However, the wide range gave ample running room for his successor, Admiral Mike Mullen, who assumed the position of chief of naval operations in July 2005—right in the midst of the third (2006) Quadrennial Defense Review. In late 2005, just before the final report was published, Admiral Mullen announced a new fleet target and associated shipbuilding plan, under which the 283 ships in commission at the end of FY 2006 would climb toward a fixed fleet target of 313 ships—an 11 percent increase in ship numbers that would take the fleet toward the upper end of the range established by Admiral Clark a year earlier.[23] For a Navy that had endured over a decade and a half of continual contraction and had faced the prospect of an even smaller 260-ship fleet, 313 ships was a target worth cheering about.

But Is It Affordable? The 313-ship battle fleet looks remarkably similar to the 302-ship fleet developed in the 1997 QDR. This should come as no surprise; it reflects a consistent requirement to fight two nearly simultaneous major combat operations, and a consistent list of combat scenarios, including a possible North Korean invasion of South Korea; a Chinese cross-strait invasion of Taiwan; and a major combat operation in the Persian Gulf involving operations against either Iraq or Iran.

Despite similarity in numbers, however, the 313-ship fleet is substantially more expensive than the earlier one. Indeed, many analysts question whether the Navy can afford to build it. For example, according to the Congressional Budget Office (CBO), the average amount of money devoted to shipbuilding between 1992 and 1999 (including nuclear carrier and submarine refuelings and complex overhauls) was about $8.9 billion annually (in FY 2007 dollars). From 2000 through 2006, the average shipbuilding budget jumped to approximately $11.7 billion annually— a 31 percent increase.[24] In comparison, the Navy projects the average annual costs to build the 313-ship Navy at approximately $14.4 billion, not counting the nuclear refueling of attack submarines and aircraft carriers. Adding in these costs raises the yearly average to approximately $15.4 billion—yet another 30-plus percent increase in projected spending. Ominously, however, the CBO estimates that the true cost of the Navy plans may actually be much higher, with average annual shipbuilding costs approaching $22 billion between FYs 2007 and 2035.[25]

Even if the Navy's lower numbers are correct, they still call for ambitious shipbuilding budget increases at a time when the long-term fiscal outlook looks to be increasingly unsettled. Reflecting uncertainties about what's ahead, Navy planners are prudently projecting a flat departmental budget topline for the foreseeable future. However, this raises an obvious question: If Navy leaders expect a relatively steady budget topline over the next thirty years, how will they free up the additional funds needed to pay for the increased shipbuilding budgets? Their answer: by generating recurring internal Navy cost-savings on the order of approximately $3 billion–$4 billion per year.

To achieve these savings, Navy leaders are making the following five key assumptions:[26]

- *Research and development (R&D) budgets will decline and stay low.* According to top Navy officials, the decline in R&D is tied to the impending shift in procurement toward a new family of ships.[27] It would be unusual, however, for R&D and procurement to diverge for any substantial length of time. Since the end of World War II, when one has gone up, so has the other. Moreover, the 2006 QDR concludes that the U.S. armed forces must begin to hedge against a serious military competition with a rising China. Given the range of potential naval challenges such a competition might spur, the assumption that R&D can be dramatically reduced and kept low is quite optimistic.

- *Personnel costs will remain flat.* The Navy has aggressive plans to reduce its overall personnel end strength with the aim of offsetting the ever-spiraling costs of manpower. Achieving this goal will often be out of the department's hands, however. For example, should Congress approve a pay raise above that requested by the Department of Defense, the Navy will be obliged to pay for it. The Navy's own FY 2007 *Unfunded Deficiency List* highlights over $250 million in such "fact-of-life" manpower cost increases.[28]

- *Fleet operations and maintenance (O&M) costs will remain flat.* The global war on terror has generated high operational demands on the Navy, exacerbating a long-standing rise in the costs to operate and maintain the fleet. Keeping O&M costs down will therefore be a challenge, as indicated by the $500 million in unfunded O&M costs found on the *Unfunded Deficiency List.*

- *Ship costs across every ship class will be contained.* Navy leaders are firmly committed to containing ship costs. Nevertheless, they readily admit that containing all cost overruns would fly in the face of actual experience; the department's record in containing ship costs is not encouraging. Nevertheless, the thirty-year shipbuilding plan depends on every single ship hitting its procurement cost target.

- *The "relief valve" in the Navy Department's overall procurement account will be the aviation procurement account.* The chief of naval operations has indicated that the shipbuilding procurement account is to be frozen to help achieve industrial stability. If any of the foregoing assumptions proves false, or if the Navy's topline decreases, the only way that shipbuilding funds can remain untouched is if the Navy makes adjustments in the aviation procurement account. However, the aviation procurement plan is also ambitious. Over the next two decades, the Navy plans to procure more variants of the F/A-18 E/F/G; hundreds of the new Joint Strike Fighter; 108 new Multimission Maritime Aircraft; hundreds of new unmanned aerial systems; and over 1,000 rotary wing aircraft. Given the wide range and scope of these programs, it seems just as likely that the aviation procurement account will steal money from shipbuilding accounts as provide procurement relief for shipbuilding.

As can be seen, then, every one of the Navy's five major assumptions is optimistic, and the likelihood that all five will simultaneously be borne out appears quite low.

Building an Affordable—and
Effective—Twenty-First-Century Battle Fleet

Simply put, the Navy will likely find it difficult to execute its current plan to build the 313-ship Navy. As a result, some Defense Department officials are urging the Navy to fundamentally change the way it designs and builds ships, and to pursue an entirely new battle fleet platform architecture that is based on larger numbers of less expensive, interconnected, manned and unmanned modular ships and platforms.[29]

While these arguments have merit, they have not been accompanied by a transition plan to get from the current fleet to the new one. It is one thing to sketch out a vision for a clean-sheet battle fleet; it is quite another to transform an existing fleet while maintaining its ability to respond to potential military contingencies. The remainder of this chapter will thus sketch out some possible modifications to the Navy's basic shipbuilding plans and outline an alternative twenty-first-century fleet that not only is affordable, but sets the Navy on a path toward a transformed fleet that can sustain American naval superiority well into the future.

While affordability is important, combat effectiveness is the key. In this regard, the Navy's battle fleet must be able to meet four key twenty-first-century operational challenges, at any point during its transformation, as derived from the overall strategic guidance found in the 2006 QDR:

- Deterring or defeating attacks against U.S. territory mounted by either state or nonstate actors, especially those involving weapons of mass destruction (WMDs);

- Supporting joint campaigns and operations in a long war against radical extremists and terrorists and the states that harbor them, and denying the sea as an operational sanctuary for these adversaries;

- Projecting power from the sea in the presence of naval anti-access/area-denial (A2/AD) networks armed with either conventional guided weapons or a small number of nuclear weapons, or both; and

- Hedging against a "disruptive" naval competition of a rising near-peer state, such as the People's Republic of China.[30]

A Strategy of the Second Move. Informed by these four existing or potential challenges, the following plan is further guided by several key judgments:

- *The top priority for Navy commanders should be to win the long war against radical extremists, terrorists, and the states that harbor them, and to prevent them from launching a catastrophic WMD attack on the United States.* Prior to 9/11, Navy thinking was that a fleet designed to fight traditional major combat operations was more than capable of handling any "lesser included" naval challenge. The ongoing global war on terror challenges that assumption, primarily because the ships and vessels needed to fight an irregular naval war generally could be smaller and, from the perspective of major combat operations, need not be as capable.

- *A near-term emphasis on irregular warfare tasks will cause no increase in risk with regard to conventional military campaigns.* The current U.S. battle fleet, operating as a component of an evolving joint multidimensional battle network, enjoys an enormous firepower advantage over any near-term traditional military or naval opponent. By 2011, each aircraft carrier in the battle force will be capable of striking over 1,000 aimpoints per day, making the maximum theoretical striking power of the Navy's ten deployable carriers a staggering 10,000 aimpoints a day. The eighty-four programmed large-surface combatants will carry among them 8,468 vertical launch system cells and an aggregate magazine capacity of approximately 9,000 battle

force missiles; the submarine fleet will add another
1,000 VLS cells.

- *The most stressing combat operations the Navy will face over
  the mid- to long-term will be those that occur in contested
  littorals—especially those protected by high-end A2/AD
  networks.* The current fleet appears capable of prevailing
  in these operations as long as it develops smart joint
  littoral warfare tactics. In this regard, the Navy and Air
  Force should develop a new doctrine for a twenty-
  first-century SeaAir Littoral Battle—similar to the way the
  Army and Air Force developed the AirLand Battle
  Doctrine in the 1980s. Just as the AirLand Battle Doctrine
  transformed the way the Army and Air Force thought
  about operations on the central front in Europe, a SeaAir
  Littoral Battle Doctrine would likely lead to entirely new
  ways of thinking about joint Navy–Air Force operations
  in twenty-first-century contested littorals.[31]

- *A key aspect of SeaAir Littoral Battle Doctrine should be the
  integration of unmanned systems into air and naval operations
  and tactics.* During the period between World Wars I and
  II, the Navy spent two decades on intense technological
  and operational experimentation trying to integrate aircraft
  into fleet operations and tactics. It will likely need to spend
  at least as long integrating unmanned aerial systems,
  unmanned surface vehicles, and unmanned underwater
  vehicles into battle fleet operations.

- *The quest for ever more capable ships is threatening to price
  the Navy out of even the 300-ship fleet market.* Recall that
  over the past two decades, the annual shipbuilding
  budget has averaged approximately $11 billion. In the
  future—assuming the Navy's own cost figures are correct—it will cost nearly $12 billion to buy just 4.25 ships:
  two *Virginia*-class SSNs (nuclear-powered attack submarines); one CG(X) (guided-missile cruiser); and one
  DDG-1000 (guided-missile destroyer); plus the amor-

tized yearly costs for a CVN-21 (nuclear-powered aircraft carrier) bought once every four years. While American shipbuilders are making remarkable strides in cutting ship production costs, U.S. warships remain very expensive due to their expansive combat systems and capabilities. If the average cost of its warships remains so high, the U.S. Navy will find it difficult to respond to a serious naval competition with a near-peer with a semicommand economy like China's.

- *To be ready to respond to any future concerted challenge, the Navy needs a robust research and development program, a dynamic and capable naval design capability, and a shipbuilding industrial base ready to surge when called upon.* However, all three of these things are currently at risk. As mentioned earlier, the Navy plans on reducing its R&D budget, and keeping it down to pay for increasing procurement budgets. Portions of the design base are already under threat. For example, for the first time in over fifty years, the United States has no new submarine in design. As a result, American submarine builders are already faced with the prospect of letting designers and engineers go. Moreover, during the next thirty years, the Navy does not plan to build more than two large surface combatants a year—barely enough work to keep two surface-combatant yards in business.

Together, these six judgments suggest that the Navy should exploit the lead it now enjoys in the global naval competition to prepare for a later bold move to reopen the lead. In other words, the Navy should adopt a naval competition strategy that might best be termed a "strategy of the second move." The following sections illustrate how such a strategy might be reflected in key components of the battle fleet. [32]

Aircraft Carriers. The Navy's large-deck aircraft carrier fleet helps to set the U.S. battle fleet apart from any other navy. Of the fifteen aircraft carriers in the world capable of launching and landing heavy fixed-wing or short take-off and arrested landing (STOAL) aircraft, the United States operates twelve.[33] Moreover, U.S. carriers are much larger than those found in other navies, carry far more capable carrier air wings, and operate as part of integrated carrier strike groups (CSGs) more powerful than any other in the world. Each CSG includes four (or more) guided-missile cruisers and destroyers, an attack submarine, and a dedicated combat logistics ship, forming a mobile strike sea base capable of projecting power out beyond a thousand miles and defending itself from attacks over, on, or under the sea.

Because carriers are so expensive to build and operate, plans to maintain the carrier fleet have a major impact on the Navy's fleet recapitalization plans. The 313-ship plan includes a requirement for eleven carriers—all nuclear-powered CVNs. The Navy will reach this goal in FY 2009 when the *USS George H. W. Bush* is commissioned, joining nine other *Nimitz*-class CVNs and the one-of-a kind *USS Enterprise*.[34] Since one of the carriers is normally in a long-term refueling and complex overhaul (RCOH), ten will be operational at any given time. The Navy plans routinely to forward-deploy two or three of its ten operational CSGs; in times of crisis, the fleet will be organized to surge a total of six within thirty days, and an additional one within ninety days.

The *Bush* will be the last of the *Nimitz*-class CVNs, which have been in serial production since 1968 and whose forty-year-old design needs updating. Accordingly, the Navy plans to begin building the first of the new CVN-21 class in FY 2008. The CVN-21 will boast impressive improvements over *Nimitz*-class carriers in its power plant, electrical distribution system, survivability, command and decision centers,[35] and aircraft sortie rates.[36] However, these new capabilities will not come cheap. The first CVN-21 will cost about $15 billion (in FY 2007 dollars), counting its nonrecurring R&D costs. Follow-on ships built between 2008 and 2035 are expected to average about $9.5 billion apiece.[37] To these must be added the costs associated with the RCOHs for older carriers—approximately $3 billion apiece. With newer carriers being built at an average rate of one every four years, and with older carriers being overhauled every three years, the Navy's 313-ship plan requires an average of approximately $3.4 billion a year for nuclear-powered aircraft carriers alone.

One recent study recommends that the Navy forgo the costs of RCOHs altogether, retiring each carrier at its midlife and building CVN-21s at a sustained rate of one every two years. While this plan would allow a faster fleet transition to the more capable CVN-21s, it would require 22 billion more shipbuilding dollars between now and 2035.[38] This plan thus seems out of reach; spending $3.4 billion a year to maintain the fleet will be tough enough.

A different option would be to shift to a combination of large and small carriers, with the larger carriers focused on operations against A2/AD networks and the smaller ones focused on long war and global war on terror operations. This approach is similar to the one taken by the U.S. Navy during World War II, when it built a mix of fast fleet carriers (CVs), light aircraft carriers (CVLs), and escort carriers (CVEs). A modern "high-low mix" would see the CVN fleet stabilize at ten carriers and nine active-duty air wings. This fleet could support two forward-deployed CSGs and could surge five carriers within thirty days and one within ninety days—sufficient force for any likely fight against a high-end naval power.

However, to make the fleet more capable of taking on an A2/AD network, the Navy should, at the same time it moves toward a 10-CVN fleet, aggressively pursue a carrier-based, unmanned aerial combat vehicle (CV-UCAS). The Navy currently views the CV-UCAS as more of a persistent intelligence, surveillance, and reconnaissance (ISR) platform. However, with their planned unrefueled range of 1,900 miles, forty-plus-hour endurance (with aerial refueling), stealthiness, and modular payload, CV-UCASs have the potential to revolutionize carrier air operations and to greatly improve the fleet's ability to take on and start to dismantle an enemy's A2/AD network from extremely long-range. This approach is consistent with a "strategy of the second move," as it will help the Navy to negate foreign A2/AD systems now in the works, such as long-range ballistic missiles with maneuverable, anti-ship warheads.

The eleventh CVN in the 313-ship plan would be replaced by four Joint Escort Carriers (J-CVEs). The plan already includes four "big-deck" LHARs—amphibious assault ships with full-length flight decks. These ships trade their floodable well decks for increased aviation capacity, enabling them to carry up to twenty-three of the short take-off and vertical landing (STOVL) versions of the new Joint Strike Fighter (JSF)—half of a larger CVN's strike fighter contingent—at a cost of approximately $2.7 billion, or 30 percent of the cost of a CVN-21.[39] By redesignating the ships as primary STOVL support platforms, the future aircraft carrier fleet would consist of ten CVNs and four J-CVEs.[40]

This flexible mix of high-low aviation power-projection plat-forms would provide more operationally available platforms than the current plan and cover the full range of expected operational challenges. It would also form the basis for a more stable and less expensive production schedule. Reducing the large-carrier require-ment to ten and building them every five years instead of every four would drop the amortized cost for big-deck carriers from $2.4 bil-lion to $1.9 billion per year. In addition, the smaller fleet would ultimately save the Navy the cost of one $9 billion CVN-21 and one $3 billion RCOH. The Navy's plan already includes three LHARs, to be built in FYs 2007, 2010, and 2013. Stabilizing the building rate of J-CVEs (and follow-on big-deck amphibious ships) at one every three years would result in the amortized costs for the ships settling at approximately $900 million a year, meaning the total recurring new construction costs for all complex aviation ships would stabi-lize at approximately $3.8 billion per year.

Submarines. The recently completed Nuclear Posture Review (NPR) set a maximum target of 1,750 submarine-launched nuclear warheads in the U.S. strategic arsenal. As a result, four *Ohio*-class strategic ballistic missile submarines (SSBNs) were removed from service and converted into conventional cruise missile and special operations transport submarines (SSGNs), each capable of carrying up to 154 Tomahawk land-attack missiles and 102 special forces troops. The result was a residual fleet of fourteen SSBNs.

Since a force of twelve *Ohio*-class SSBNs appears sufficient to meet the nuclear deterrent requirements outlined in the NPR,[41] two more SSBNs could conceivably be converted to SSGNs during their scheduled midlife engineering and refueling overhauls. Such a move would serve two purposes. First, it would help maintain the submarine design base, as the conversions would require a modest additional engineering effort.[42] Second, it would increase the fleet's stealth strike power. Two additional SSGNs would give the SSGN fleet a total of 924 stealth VLS cells—the equivalent strike capacity of over eleven DDG-1000s, the Navy's new stealthy—and expensive—surface warship.

The eighteen SSBNs and SSGNs are to be replaced starting in the 2020s by a new, undefined "SSXN"—a hull designed from the outset to serve in either the nuclear or conventional role. The Navy is currently debating whether to accelerate the design work on this submarine to help maintain the undersea design base.

Compared to the SSBN force, the attack-submarine force presents a difficult force structure and industrial base problem. After the Soviet Union imploded, the Navy began to reduce its large SSN force toward an eventual target of fifty boats, set in the 1997 QDR. At the same time, it decided to shift serial production from its ultimate Cold War SSN, the *Seawolf*—a fast, deep-diving, and extremely quiet boat optimized for open-ocean and under-ice anti-submarine warfare—to a new SSN optimized for littoral warfare operations. As the new submarine—now known as the *Virginia*, or SSN-774, class—was being designed, the Navy did not authorize a single new SSN for a period of six years (FY 2092–97). Moreover, although the Navy originally planned to build one *Virginia* per year between FYs 1998 and 2001 and then shift to a sustained building rate of two per year,[43] higher than expected unit costs and lower than expected shipbuilding budgets caused it to postpone the shift until FY 2012, and then only if the unit costs could be reduced from the current $2.5 billion to $2.0 billion per boat.

The upshot of all of these decisions is that the bottom will fall out of the attack-submarine fleet during the 2020s as the SSNs built during the late Cold War reach the end of their thirty-three-year expected service lives (ESLs). Should the Navy continue to build *Virginias* at a rate of one per year, the SSN fleet would fall to as few as twenty-eight boats in FY 2028 and stabilize thereafter at thirty-three boats—far below the fleet requirement of forty-eight SSNs. This circumstance is especially troubling given recent improvements in the Chinese submarine fleet. Although the People's Liberation Army Navy has long operated a sizeable fleet of some fifty to seventy submarines, until recently the majority of them were obsolescent diesel-electric boats. Starting in the 1990s, the PLAN began a qualitative upgrade of its conventional submarine fleet, buying an eventual total of twelve Russian *Kilo*-class submarines and shifting into serial production of two new indigenous designs known as the *Song* and the *Yuan* classes. Additionally, it began production of a new Type 093 SSN and a new Type 094 SSBN, both great improvements over first-generation PLAN nuclear boats. All of the new attack boats are capable of launching anti-ship cruise missiles, including the deadly supersonic SSN-27 Sizzler, while submerged.[44]

At the very least, the replacement of outdated submarines with modern boats will make future Chinese A2/AD networks increasingly lethal. No one knows, however, exactly what the Chinese intend to do after replacing their older boats. One analyst projects that, because of expected retirements of older boats, the Chinese submarine fleet will grow from sixty-eight to seventy-four submarines by 2010.[45] What then? Will China continue to expand its submarine fleet, or will it maintain a force of about the same size? No one is certain. The Navy must therefore be fully prepared to compete against a greatly improved PLAN submarine fleet and capable of responding to a major fleet expansion.

How best to respond? One option is to proceed as planned, shifting to two *Virginias* per year in FY 2012, and building a total of thirty through 2020. Presently, the Navy intends to shift production to an improved version of the *Virginia*, maintaining a steady-state production rate of two boats per year through FY 2028, and thereafter shifting to a 1-2-1-2 building profile. This plan results in a fleet of forty SSNs in FY 2029 and fifty-two in FY 2037; thereafter, the fleet settles to its steady-state requirement of forty-eight SSNs.

However, it also results in a fourteen-year force structure trough during which the Navy will be below its attack-boat requirement. Some critics therefore argue that the Navy should shift to two boats per year as early as FY 2009. However, since this move would add only three additional boats to the basic plan and reduce the force structure trough to eleven years, it appears of questionable value given that, barring a precipitous increase in the Chinese submarine fleet, a forty-SSN force should be more than capable of holding its own. This is so because U.S. attack-submariners have always emphasized quality over quantity in undersea combat. For example, in 1990, as the Cold War was coming to a close, the U.S. attack-submarine force believed it could defeat a combined Soviet submarine fleet of 264 total boats with its 93 SSNs. In other words, it willingly accepted a force ratio of 1.00 U.S. boat for every 2.84 Soviet submarines.[46] This suggests the PLAN submarine fleet would have to double to a total of 113 boats before the U.S. SSN fleet faced more stressing force ratios than those it accepted during the Cold War. So, until PLAN intentions are better understood, a submarine-building plan that results in a forty-boat force in FY 2029 should be adequate.

Indeed, a more pressing concern is that we appear to be on the verge of a shift to a new undersea warfighting regime. Fought primarily in littoral waters, it will likely be marked by the appearance of undersea battle networks composed of ubiquitous sensors; manned, air-independent submarines (both conventional and nuclear); smaller manned underwater vehicles (MUVs); and increasingly capable unmanned underwater vehicles (UUVs). In this new regime, comparisons of submarine force ratios will tell only part of the story; a smaller submarine force that has an advantage in undersea surveillance and UUV tactics may prevail against a much larger force of manned submarines, especially in confined littoral waters.[47]

The United States has dominated the current underwater warfighting regime; it cannot afford not to dominate the next. Accelerating efforts to prepare for the new undersea regime and maintaining a viable submarine design and industrial base appear far more important than moving to two submarines per year in FY 2009. Moreover, the next undersea warfighting system should probably not be merely an improvement on the *Virginia*, which was designed during an undersea regime dominated by nuclear attack boats. Instead, the Navy should seek a clean-sheet solution—one specifically designed as part of an undersea combat network including MUVs and UUVs.

Consistent with this thinking, an alternative approach to the 313-ship plan would be to build ten *Virginias* between FYs 2012 and 2018 instead of the fourteen now planned (that is, a 2-1-2-1-2-1-1 profile), and to divert some of the money saved to a design effort for an entirely new modular undersea warfighting system (UWS) with large amounts of internal volume capable of employing numerous MUVs and UUVs. The aim of this effort would be to introduce a new UWS in FY 2018 that could be built in four years rather than the six years now required to build a *Virginia*, at 80–90 percent of its cost.

Under this plan, the Navy would be positioned to respond more quickly to any concerted Chinese undersea challenge in the 2020s. First, it would keep U.S. engineers busy until they were needed to design the aforementioned SSXN. Indeed, the design effort might allow the Navy to combine the UWS and SSXN efforts, leading to a common hull for future SSN, SSGN, and SSBN missions, and lowering unit costs for all variants. Second, if the USW could be built in four years by ramping up to a sustained rate of two boats per year in FY 2019, the tactical submarine fleet would number no less than forty-one boats in FY 2028 and would reach the overall target of fifty-two boats in FY 2036—numbers comparable with the current plan. By anticipating and actively seeking to shape the nature of the emerging undersea warfighting regime, the Navy should be able to block any future Chinese undersea challenge. Additionally, by cutting the unit production costs of UWSs, the Navy could more easily ramp up production if a Chinese threat required that the U.S. attack-submarine fleet be increased above forty-eight boats.

Like the Navy's plan, this alternative plan entails some risk. Should the PLAN continue its frenetic production pace and rapidly expand its fleet much beyond the sixty-eight boats in the midterm, it may calculate it can take on and beat the static U.S. submarine fleet. Additionally, although the U.S. SSN fleet will remain above fifty boats through FY 2017, the average age of these boats will be much greater than those of the PLAN fleet. Therefore, should the Navy receive more shipbuilding money than expected, its first priority should be to buy additional submarines.

Small Surface Combatants and Mine-Warfare Vessels. Since World War II, small combatants have played a limited role in the U.S. surface fleet.[48] While preparing for a possible war against the Soviet Navy, the U.S. Navy emphasized large, multimission ships capable of defending themselves and high-value units such as aircraft carriers and battleships against high-speed submarine, missile, and air attack. Thus, except when forced to do so by actual wartime requirements—such as patrolling the coast and rivers of Vietnam—the Navy steered away from small combatants except those designed specifically to support naval special-warfare units or to hunt for and neutralize mines.

With the Cold War won, the Navy announced in 1992 that it would shift the focus of its operations from the open ocean to shallow and congested littoral waters—the natural stomping ground for small combatants. This move suggested a possible renaissance for small surface ships. However, for the surface-warfare community, the true shift in focus was simply from engaging targets at sea to targets on land, and for this mission the Navy still preferred large surface combatants with large magazine capacities. For example, after the 1997 QDR set a surface-combatant target of 116 ships, the Navy announced it would replace its remaining 4,000-ton guided-missile frigates with 16,000-ton DD-21 land-attack destroyers! Additionally, it gave up its riverine warfare mission to the Marine Corps, and although it built fourteen small patrol coastal boats for naval special-warfare support, by 2000 the Navy planned to transfer all of them to either the Coast Guard or foreign navies.

With the declaration of the global war on terror, small combatants are making a comeback. The Navy has reembraced the riverine mission, planning three squadrons of twelve boats by FY 2008. It has retained eight of its 330-ton patrol coastal combatants, and plans to retrieve the five it lent to the Coast Guard after 9/11. However, the big news is that the Navy now intends to replace its thirty residual guided-missile frigates and twenty-six mine-warfare craft with fifty-five new littoral-combat ships (LCSs)—fast, shallow draft ships of about 2,800 tons full load displacement. The Navy plans to authorize and build an average of six LCSs a year from FY 2009 to FY 2016, and reach its requirement for fifty-five ships by FY 2018.

The LCS is a new type of warship, built from the keel up to act as a flexible component in future naval battle networks. It has a large amount of internal reconfigurable volume that can be rapidly changed to accommodate different mission modules. The ship was originally trumpeted as a counter-A2/AD platform, capable of carrying modules designed to combat quiet diesel submarines, mines, and swarming boats—serious threats in close-in littoral waters. These missions remain important in Navy planning.[49] Recently, however, the Navy has begun to describe its residual frigates and future LCSs primarily in terms of requirements for the global war on terror.[50] This makes sense, since the LCSs are relatively cheap to procure (approximately $297 million for the basic hull, not counting mission modules) and cheap to operate (because they have small crews). Moreover, by virtue of their speed and shallow draft, they are perfectly suited for irregular naval warfare tasks, such as maritime intercept operations, choke point patrols, special operations support, and counterpiracy operations.

In addition to building a new small combatant for the global war on terror, the Navy is contemplating establishing five global fleet stations that would establish a long-lasting regional naval presence and be the focal point for long-war naval operations.[51] To improve the on-station time of LCSs assigned to the global fleet stations, the Navy intends to assemble four crews for every three of the ships and to conduct sea swaps—or crew rotations—on ships kept on station. This system will provide a minimum of 40 percent more presence days than a single-crewed LCS fleet. In other words, fifty-five multi-crewed LCSs will provide the same number of presence days as approximately seventy-seven single-crewed LCSs.[52]

The 313-ship plan authorizes the last of fifty-five LCSs in FY 2016. The Navy would not build another for fourteen years, suggesting that it is expecting twenty-five years of service out of each LCS. Given the high usage rates the Navy plans for these ships, this expectation seems optimistic. Indeed, given that the LCS will be the primary combatant for the long war, one might expect the force to suffer attrition through battle losses or accident. A better plan might therefore be to lock in the LCS build rate at four ships per year and to maintain that rate over time. Although the Navy would not hit its inventory goal of fifty-five ships until FY 2022, four years later than planned, the shortfall would be offset to some degree by the residual mine-warfare vessels that will remain in the fleet through FY 2024. This scheme would better maintain the Navy's small-combatant industrial base and, with the introduction of periodic new LCS designs, it would also better maintain the small-combatant design base.

With a twenty-five-year service life, a sustained build rate of four ships per year would result in a steady-state LCS fleet of 100 ships without intervention. The Navy could choose to allow the fleet to grow beyond the fifty-five planned ships to meet greater than expected requirements; to place excess ships in reserve or transfer them to the Coast Guard; or to sell or transfer the excess ships to foreign allied navies. Any of these choices would contribute to winning an irregular naval war.

Large Surface Combatants. The last of sixty-two authorized *Arleigh Burke*-class DDGs will be commissioned in 2011. When combined with the twenty-two remaining *Ticonderoga*-class CGs, the Navy will have a total of eighty-four large, multimission surface combatants against a stated requirement of eighty-eight. Each of these ships will be equipped with the powerful AEGIS combat system.[53] Additionally, as discussed earlier, the ships will carry over 8,400 VLS cells and an additional four hundred–plus Harpoon anti-ship cruise missiles.

These eighty-four ships will comprise the most powerful surface-battle line in the world. It will also be a young one. Commissioned from 1986 through 2011, the average age of the fleet will be only thirteen years. With expected service lives of thirty-five years, the eighty-four AEGIS ships will comprise the heart of the battle fleet for the next two decades.

In 1997, the Navy planned on augmenting its eighty-four planned AEGIS ships (at that time, the mix was to be twenty-seven *Ticonderogas* and fifty-seven *Burkes*) with thirty-two DD-21s, built from FY 2004 to FY 2015 at an average target price of $1.1 billion per hull (in FY 2007 dollars).[54] In FY 2015, large-combatant production would then shift to the CG-21, the expected replacement for the *Ticonderoga*-class CGs. The current plan is different and more expensive. It bolsters the sixty-two-ship DDG fleet with seven new 14,500-ton DDG-1000s starting in FY 2007, and begins production of nineteen new CG(X)s built on the DDG-1000 hull in FY 2011, five years earlier than planned. Unfortunately, however, given their high projected average procurement costs ($2.7 billion–$2.8 billion), the Navy expects to authorize only seven DDG-1000s and six CG(X)s between FYs 2007 and 2016, at an average rate of 1.3 ships per year, before settling on a sustained build rate of 2.0 CG(X)s per year between FYs 2017 and 2022.

In FY 2023, the Navy would build the final CG(X) and one new DDG(X)—the first of a new class of ships expected to replace the sixty-two *Burke* DDGs after 2026. Thereafter, although the *Burkes* were commissioned between 1991 and 2011 at an average rate of three ships per year, the Navy's plan still calls for only two surface combatants per year. Assuming future ships will serve a full thirty-five-year ESL, a sustained build rate of two ships per year will result in a steady-state surface combatant fleet of only seventy ships—eighteen ships (20 percent) below the Navy's stated requirement for eighty-eight guided-missile cruisers and destroyers.

The Navy is anxious to shift production from the less expensive legacy *Burke*-class DDG to the new DDG-1000/CG(X) class of ships to introduce improved fleet combat capabilities, including a stealthy hull; a new, all-electric integrated propulsion and power system; and increased automation resulting in smaller crew sizes. While each of these advances has merit, they do not clearly justify the Navy's surface-combatant recapitalization plans, especially its plan to spend nearly $20 billion on seven DDG-1000s.

In this regard, the Navy judges the *Burke* to be a better open-ocean air defender and the DDG-1000 a better littoral air defender. It considers the two ships roughly equal in anti–cruise missile capabilities, depending on the threat and scenario, and equally capable ASW platforms.[55] While the stealthier DDG-1000 will be more survivable, it is questionable whether that survivability is worth an additional $1 billion or more per hull. Similarly, although its new six-inch guns and VLS will provide added fleet strike capability, as discussed earlier, strike power is one thing this fleet does not lack. In any event, a comparison between the DDG-1000 and the *Burke* is a false one. The real comparison should be made between the incremental battle network improvement between an eighty-eight-ship surface-battle line, which includes seven DDG-1000s, and one containing eighty-eight modernized and updated AEGIS/VLS combatants. Given planned improvements that will help cover existing network gaps or capability shortfalls, it is hard to make the case that $20 billion spent for seven powerful new DDGs will result in a dramatically improved overall fleet battle capability. The aforementioned increase of the SSGN fleet to six boats provides a case in point. For an incremental cost of less than $1 billion, the Navy will be able to maintain the equivalent missile strike capacity of seven DDG-1000s forward-deployed at all times, on even stealthier platforms.

Similarly, while the new electric power system and advanced crew automation techniques are important innovations that should be pursued, neither is linked to the 14,000-ton DDG-1000 hull. The new British Type 45 guided-missile destroyer, a ship nearly half the displacement of the DDG-1000, will also have an integrated electric drive and power system and a crew of only 190. It is the DDG-1000's technologies, and not the ship itself, that will provide the fleet with the biggest operational payoff. Navy officers are fond of comparing the DDG-1000 to the British Navy's *HMS Dreadnought*, whose commissioning in 1906 made all previous battleships obsolete and affected the building of all battleships thereafter. What they forget is that the *Dreadnought* was a class of one ship.[56] Two DDG-1000s, built in the two different surface combatant yards, could serve the same purpose as the *Dreadnought*— technology demonstrator for the future fleet.[57]

Some might argue that not shifting immediately to the DDG-1000 and CG(X) will mean higher fleet manning requirements and manpower costs. But this argument is not as compelling at it first sounds. Because the Navy plans to modernize all eighty-four of its AEGIS/VLS combatants and keep them all in service for thirty-five years, the seven DD(X)s and first three CG(X)s will generate additional fleet manpower demands through the early 2020s. Indeed, the Navy's plan will see the surface-combatant fleet jump to ninty-five ships (seven over requirement) in FY 2020–21 before trending down to eighty-eight ships in FY 2027. As a result, the shift to the new ships will result in little or no total fleet manpower savings until the mid-2020s. By replacing AEGIS/VLS ships as they retire in the 2020s and 2030s with new combatants with smaller crews, the Navy would see essentially the same manpower savings it will accrue with its current 313-ship plan.

Indeed, there is only one truly compelling argument for building the DDG-1000 and CG(X) as planned: the Navy cannot wait to build the *Ticonderoga*-class replacement, because a ten-year delay in building the next large surface warship would effectively sound the death knell for the large-combatant industrial base. There are, however, potentially far less expensive ways to keep the industrial base hot. One approach would be to build just two DDG-1000 technology demonstrators, and to continue the *Burke* production line at a minimum sustaining rate of one per year, starting in FY 2008, for a period of seven years. This would meet the current fleet requirement of sixty-nine operational DDGs called for in the Navy's 313-ship plan. The costs for these ships would be offset, to some degree, by decommissioning the three oldest *Ticonderoga*-class cruisers (or the cruisers in the worst material condition). These moves would create the planned baseline fleet of nineteen CGs and sixty-nine DDGs.

Some of the money saved would be used to jumpstart a design effort for a new class of large battle network combatants (LBNCs), built along the lines pioneered by the LCS—with a sea frame capable of accepting a CG, DDG, or DD (destroyer) combat system. The aim would be to build the first ship of this class in 2016, with a not-to-exceed average cost for follow-on ships of $1.8 billion per ship in FY 2007 dollars (the target cost for the future DDG(X)). The plan would be to build five ships every two years beginning in FY 2017, which would lead to a long-term steady-state fleet of eighty-eight LBNCs.

This plan is similar to the one proposed for the SSN fleet. It exploits the lead the U.S. surface fleet now enjoys by pursuing a game-changing surface-combatant design in the next decade. It also helps maintain the design base in the near-term and the industrial base in the mid- to long-term.

The Expeditionary Warfare Fleet. In contrast, the Navy's plans for a game-changing design for its expeditionary warfare fleet would be slowed and modified. Just after the Cold War ended, Navy and Marine officers concluded that the battle force should maintain an amphibious landing force capable of lifting three Marine expeditionary brigades (MEBs). The Secretary of the Navy subsequently approved a "fiscally constrained" 2.5-MEB lift requirement. Together with three maritime prepositioning force squadrons (MPFs), the battle fleet entered the 1990s with a requirement to support the employment and deployment of 5.5 MEBs—a target subsequently approved in the 1997 QDR.[58]

In contrast, the 313-ship fleet includes a requirement for thirty-one amphibious warships capable of carrying approximately 1.9 MEBs; twelve new future maritime prepositioning force (MPF(F)) ships capable of sea-basing 1.0 MEB and logistically supporting that MEB and an additional combat brigade ashore; and eight additional "noncountable" legacy MPF(E) ships—two to support the MPF(F) squadron, and a six-ship squadron to carry the equipment for a single MEB. Because of the high projected costs to reconstitute MEB equipment sets after Marines withdraw from Iraq, Marine planners have apparently concluded they can only afford to reconstitute two MEB sets. In essence, then, the new plan represents a 30 percent reduction in total maneuver lift, falling from the 1997 5.5 MEB goal to only 3.9 MEBs.

Defenders of the plan often tout the development of the MPF(F) squadron as one of the most transformational components of the fleet put forth in the 2006 QDR, and one well worth the overall reduction in expeditionary maneuver capacity. However, the development of the MPF(F) is a case study in how questionable assumptions drive questionable programs. The move to substitute commercial MPF(F) ships for amphibious warships was driven by a new joint requirement to be able to perform a forcible-entry operation in ten to fourteen days. This requirement was derived from the so-called "10-30-30" metric, which called for a joint force capable of seizing the initiative in a first war within ten days; swiftly defeating the enemy in thirty days; and taking thirty days before repeating the process in another theater against a second adversary.[59]

There is just one problem: "10-30-30" is completely out of tune with the post–9/11 world, in which the likelihood of traditional campaigns is receding. Moreover, adopting any metric that helps to inculcate a short-war mentality in an era of irregular foes, regional powers armed with nuclear weapons, and near-peer competitors with advanced A2/AD systems is asking for trouble.

Nevertheless, the requirement to inject a single brigade from the sea in ten to fourteen days drove the subsequent development and design of the MPF(F) concept and squadron. Because most of the fleet's amphibious landing ships were home-based in ports in the United States, a large amphibious task force could not be assembled in a forward theater in much less than thirty days. An MPF(F) squadron, anchored in forward theaters, could arrive anywhere off the coast of the Eurasian landmass much closer to the ten-day "seize the initiative" requirement in "10-30-30."

Unfortunately, the costs for a single twelve-ship MPF(F) squadron grew to nearly $15 billion, not counting the $1 billion high-speed ship necessary to carry the Marines' non-self-deploying helicopters to the sea base.[60] Given the competing demands in the budget, something had to give. The 313-ship fleet thus includes only one new MPF(F) squadron (the Marines had argued for two), and only one legacy MPF(E) squadron. Moreover, although the 313-ship fleet includes a requirement for thirty-one amphibious warships, its supporting thirty-year shipbuilding plan only builds thirty, and three of these are earmarked to support long-war tasks. The resulting amphibious fleet thus cannot support the landing of a two-MEB force—a force that both Navy and Marine officers had long judged to be the minimum for forcible-entry operations. To obtain a force this size, the amphibious ships will need to be augmented by the MPF(F) squadron. In other words, both the future amphibious and MPF fleets will be less capable than at any time in the past. This diminution in battle fleet maneuver capacity does not seem to make sense in an era that is characterized by diminished overseas access as well as widely dispersed ground combat operations against an elusive, irregular foe.

In sum, current plans for the expeditionary warfare fleet are overly focused on speed of reaction, rest upon a sea-basing concept largely unsupported by operational testing, and underestimate the flexibility that amphibious landing ships provide the fleet in an ongoing long war. Indeed, data compiled by the Center for Naval Analyses indicate that while aircraft carriers were the platforms most often called upon during crises in the Cold War, amphibious landing ships were most in demand during the 1990s.[61] These data make perfect sense: A ship that is capable of operating boats, landing craft, and helicopters and of transporting and supporting intact maneuver units, and is equipped with onboard cranes, medical, and command and control facilities, is perfectly suited for a variety of operational tasks on both the seaward and landward sides of the world's coastlines. Moreover, amphibious landing ships remain the most efficient means to transport intact combat units over transoceanic distances. They are, therefore, the best platforms for both amphibious patrolling and forcible-entry missions.

Accordingly, the $15 billion–$16 billion currently earmarked to build the MPF(F) squadron might be better spent on upgrading the amphibious landing fleet and modifying the legacy MPF fleet in order to improve the battle fleet's irregular warfare capabilities. In the long war, building an expeditionary warfare fleet capable of forming many distributed micro–sea bases appears to be a better strategy than forming one large sea base optimized for traditional power-projection operations. Moreover, retaining a robust amphibious fleet will provide a hedge against the possibility that the battle fleet may once again be called upon to seize operational access for the joint force. During the Cold War—an era of assured access—the battle fleet never had an amphibious lift requirement for less than three MEBs, and this target was reaffirmed in the early post–Cold War period.[62] Now, with far fewer bases overseas and forward access increasingly uncertain, prudence dictates that the battle fleet must retain a minimal capability to seize a forward lodgment under conditions of contested access.

In light of this, an alternative plan would be to extend the LPD-17 program, which is currently scheduled to stop after a nine-ship buy. According to the plan, the Navy would continue to buy one LPD-17 per year through FY 2024, building toward a target fleet of twenty-four ships. The first batch of twelve LPD-17s would replace the eleven LPDs currently in service; the second batch of twelve would replace the twelve LSDs now in the fleet on a one-for-one basis. This plan serves several purposes. First, it would help maintain the industrial base for medium-sized amphibious ships over the near- to mid-term. Second, replacement of the LSDs before the end of their forty-year service lives would allow them to be used in other battle fleet roles. Third, by recapitalizing the LSD fleet earlier than now planned, the Navy would free up procurement money in the late 2020s, currently earmarked for replacing the LSDs, to help pay for recapitalizing the SSN, SSBN, and SSGN fleets.

Along with four J-CVEs and eight big-deck LHD amphibious assault ships (a twelve-ship fleet built at a sustained rate of one every three years), this alternative amphibious landing fleet would provide the same 2.9 MEBs of sea based lift found in the 313-ship fleet. However, because this lift would be found exclusively on amphibious ships, the Marines could retain two legacy MPF squadrons, meaning the combined expeditionary warfare fleet would be able to deploy and employ 4.9 MEBs, rather than 3.9 MEBs. The third MPF squadron could be modified to serve as sea-based support ships. These modified ships would serve two roles. Separately, they would be used to support special operations forces or small infantry units involved in long-war operations along the Eurasian and African littoral. Together, they would perform the logistical support role so important to the sea-basing concept.

In other words, for about the same $15 billion–$16 billion now planned, the battle fleet would improve its ability to support the long war, conduct forcible-entry operations, and logistically support joint forces operating ashore from a sea base.

An Affordable, Transformed Fleet

As this discussion hopefully highlights, there are ready ways in which the Navy can set the battle fleet on a course far less fiscally risky and far more effective in solving the near- to mid-term challenges associated with the long war, and the potential long-term challenges of dealing with a rising China or confronting future A2/AD networks in contested littorals. The illustrative plan laid out in these pages exploits the lead the Navy now enjoys in the global naval competition but also lays the necessary groundwork for a move to meet more serious challenges as they present themselves. This would entail spending less money on most planned new ships, and more money on testing, experimentation, and design and industrial base maintenance.

In every battle network component, this plan opens avenues that may radically alter the character of the future fleet. With regard to aircraft carriers, it reintroduces a mix of large and small carriers that provides more flexibility and more aviation platforms to fight the long war. In addition, it anticipates a shift toward more unmanned carrier strike aircraft that may ultimately improve the fleet's ability to fight in the face of advanced A2/AD networks. With regard to submarines, the plan aims to anticipate and prepare for a possible shift in the undersea warfighting regime, seeking a new platform designed to operate within new undersea combat networks that include smaller manned and unmanned underwater vehicles, and one that perhaps can be used for the SSN, SSBN, and SSGN missions For surface combatants, the plan forgoes the expensive DDG-1000 and diverts money toward an entirely new large battle network combatant built along the design principles of the LCS—that is, an affordable modular sea frame capable of handling CG, DDG, and DD combat systems. As for the expeditionary warfare fleet, the plan seeks to delay a radical move to a new MPF(F) squadron until the concept is more thoroughly tested, and instead improve the battle forces' ability to fight the long war and to create forward access when it is either denied or contested.

For those obsessed with ship counts, the resulting fleet is very similar to the Navy's planned 313-ship fleet. It maintains eighteen SSBNs and SSGNs, although in a different mix, with twelve SSBNs and six SSGNs. It builds toward an SSN force target of forty-eight boats, a large surface-combatant target of eighty-eight ships, and a small surface-combatant target of fifty-five LCSs. The expeditionary warfare fleet would drop from forty-three "countable" ships (thirty-one amphibious landing ships and twelve MPF(F) ships) to thirty-two countable amphibious ships. However, the total number of expeditionary warfare ships, including noncountable legacy MPF ships, would only drop from fifty-one to forty-eight. These losses are made up for by three additional aircraft carriers (ten CVNs and four J-CVEs instead of eleven CVNs). Although not covered here, depending on decisions regarding the fleet's combat logistics force ships (ships designed to replenish U.S. warships at sea) and other support ships like tenders, tugs, and high-speed vessels, the fleet might actually increase in size. Of course, not included in this number are the more than 150 small combatants found in the U.S. Coast Guard, the Navy's joint partner in fighting the long war and preventing attacks on the U.S. homeland.

Despite being similar in size, this fleet is far less expensive to procure, especially in the near- to mid-term:

- It requires a steady-state investment of $3.8 billion a year to maintain a fleet of ten CVNs, four J-CVEs, and eight LHDs/LHDXs. Over time, the plan saves the cost of a $9 billion CVN-21 as well as a $3 billion refueling and complex overhaul for an older carrier.

- It converts two additional SSBNs into SSGNs, but builds three fewer *Virginias* between now and FY 2018. The savings are used to accelerate plans for the *Virginia* follow-on—a new undersea warfighting system—by two years, and to create savings over the long term by designing a more affordable and producible system.

- It builds only two DDG-1000s as technology demonstrators, trading the $13.5 billion–plus needed to build the remaining ships for seven perfectly capable *Arleigh Burke* DDGs and the design of a new large battle network combatant designed to recapitalize the eighty-eight-ship AEGIS/VLS fleet in the 2020s.

- It builds fifty-five LCSs, albeit at a slower but sustained rate, in the process saving procurement funds, maintaining the small-combatant industrial base, and giving the Navy flexibility during the 2020s either to expand its own small-combatant fleet or build partner capacity by transferring excess LCSs to either the Coast Guard or allies.

- It diverts the $15 billion–$16 billion earmarked for the MPF(F) squadron into a sustained building program for LPD-17s, in the process building up amphibious lift, sustaining the amphibious-warship industrial base, and freeing up older LSDs for conversion into other battle fleet roles.

This plan also establishes sustainable steady-state production profiles for CVN-21s; J-CVEs; big deck amphibious ships; medium-sized amphibious ships; attack submarines; and large and small battle network combatants. Moreover, by recapitalizing the amphibious fleet early and spending the money now to design cheaper undersea warfighting platforms and large battle network combatants, the plan works to relieve the pressure on high shipbuilding costs now expected in the 2020s, when the Navy plans to buy the SSXN and the new DDGX, continue to build SSNs, and recapitalize the amphibious landing fleet.

Is this plan perfect? Of course not. It was developed to demonstrate three things. First, barring a major change in the global competitive environment, a 300-ship Navy should be sufficient for the nation's needs. Second, without these changes, even a "300-ship Navy" is probably not affordable. And third, rather than seeking to widen its current lead, the Navy would be much better off positioning itself to make bolder moves in the years ahead when new numbers and capabilities will be required.

5

The Marine Corps: A Hybrid Force for a Hybrid World

Francis G. Hoffman

The 2006 Quadrennial Defense Review (QDR) should have provided the Marine Corps with a coherent map to train, equip, and organize forces for the world it faces today and the one it will face in the future. It didn't.

On its face, the QDR was a well-constructed report, with clear prose that identified four clear priorities: defeating terrorist networks; defending the homeland in depth; shaping the choices of countries at "strategic crossroads"; and preventing hostile states and nonstate actors from acquiring or using weapons of mass destruction.[1]

And, indeed, the QDR's final report shares many of the themes and priorities identified in General Mike Hagee's vision for the Marine Corps of the twenty-first century, as published in the July 2005 issue of the *Marine Corps Gazette*.[2] In particular, it underscores the increased salience of irregular warfare and the need to increase the flexibility of military forces across the entire spectrum of conflict. The report also explicitly supports key themes that are central to Marine concepts and development efforts, including seabasing, expeditionary forces, strategic mobility, and rapid operational maneuver. Nevertheless, the QDR fails in critical respects when it comes to the Marine Corps, either by misunderstanding what is required to tackle the priorities it lists or by altogether failing to address specific concerns.

First, despite the review's acknowledgment that our overwhelming military strength motivates future competitors to seek unique asymmetric approaches to overcome it, the QDR fails to follow through with its own logic. Having suggested that both state and nonstate actors will employ unconventional tactics to erode American will and increase the costs of U.S. military operations, the report narrowly confines U.S. response to this emerging phenomenon to counterterrorism and the defeat of terrorist networks, to be accomplished through an increased reliance on special operations forces (SOF) and so-called "indirect approaches." Moreover, even while claiming to give greater emphasis to the global war on terror and irregular warfare activities—including long-duration unconventional warfare, counterterrorism, counterinsurgency, and military support for stabilization and reconstruction efforts—with the exception of a single statement regarding the adaptation of Army and Marine "general purpose" forces to deal with these problems, the report focuses almost entirely on SOF and Special Operations Command (SOCOM) in areas addressing them—while at the same time reducing rather than increasing the size of the Marine Corps.

Overall, the report underestimates the impact of what others have dubbed the "counterrevolution in military affairs" (Counter RMA), or what I called the rise of "complex irregular warfare," as the most likely form of warfare for the foreseeable future.[3] The Counter RMA represents the expected response of future antagonists to our own information superiority. Rather than present easy targets for American sensors and airpower, America's adversaries will employ modern technologies in unconventional ways and use irregular tactics to target U.S. vulnerabilities and erode America's political will. Due to the diffusion of advanced technologies and the information revolution, future opponents will be more capable than irregular foes of the past. Classical counterinsurgency techniques will have to be updated to address this more sophisticated and complex adversary.

Similarly, the QDR claims to have developed a new paradigm when it comes to planning a force structure that will "make adjustments to better capture the realities of a long war."[4] This new construct is indeed more sophisticated than the previous paradigm, which used as its baseline the scenario of handling two nearly simultaneous major regional contingencies. In theory, the new model—

which is sometimes described as the "Michelin Man," due to its three overlapping components of homeland defense, the global war on terror, and conventional campaigns—should determine both the *size* and *shape* of the military force structure. Instead, it leaves unclear exactly how it will do so with regard to the Marine Corps and fails to explain how today's force will evolve into tomorrow's.

Furthermore, the report observes that, "for the foreseeable future, steady-state operations, including operations as part of a long war against terrorist networks, and associated rotation base and sustainment requirements, will be the main determinant for sizing U.S forces."[5] If that were the case, one would have hoped for a reversal of previous pressures from the Office of the Secretary of Defense (OSD) to cut ground forces, and an acknowledgment that changes in the security environment require fresh thinking on this front. Instead, the publication of the QDR resulted in a programmatic decision to reduce end strength in all the services—in the case of the Marine Corps, by cutting some 5,000 troops. The formal requirement for sizing U.S. forces seems to have been undercut by economic constraints and a general misunderstanding about the heavy manpower requirements needed to sustain military activities around the globe. In spite of its new Michelin Man model, the QDR continues the Pentagon's penchant for giving the greatest weight to preexisting conventional military requirements and too little to the manpower-intensive irregular wars we are now fighting and will likely be fighting in the years ahead.

The QDR also underemphasizes key Marine capabilities—namely, forcible entry and urban warfare. These oversights do not square well with aspects of the report that highlight the need to secure access to vital areas of the world, the growing technological sophistication of states who may desire to thwart American plans to do so, and the reality of global demographics, which suggest that future conflicts will predominantly occur in densely populated urban complexes.

Although the QDR emphasizes the need to maintain "enduring U.S. advantages in operational maneuver" and project force "from all domains to facilitate access,"[6] its emphasis on the "indirect approach," "lines of least resistance," and "lines of least expectation"[7] suggest that some within the Pentagon continue to equate amphibious warfare with frontal and bloody assaults like that on Tarawa in World War II. In doing so, they ignore the work of the Marine Corps over the past decade to develop "over-the-horizon" assault concepts emphasizing operational reach, speed, and agility.[8] The ability to take the line of least expectation often requires the operational maneuver and reach afforded by potent amphibious forces. Lest anyone forget, the landing at Inchon—the last major amphibious operation in wartime—was a brilliant end-run that was both unexpected and directed at a line of least resistance. Operational creativity is no substitute for operational capacity; in fact, it is the latter which makes the former possible. When capacity is insufficient, the enemy easily identifies the sole executable line of operation, and creates a corresponding defense of maximum resistance.

The report is also silent with respect to urban warfare. Here again, wishful thinking may be the culprit. By emphasizing the role of indirect approaches and indigenous partners, we continue to deny the brutish and enduring realities of human conflict. The Defense Department's leadership is creating a strategy for heroes, a world in which extreme sacrifices will ultimately have to be made in order to overcome our rigid adherence to warfighting theories that do not match the realities of ground warfare.[9]

The employment of more indirect approaches, including stealth and flexible basing, and building up the strength of partners and allies, is also proposed by the QDR as means to increase both strategic and operational freedom of action.[10] Given the emphasis on operational freedom, the report could have been expected to set clearer priorities for funding and manning powerful amphibious forces to provide persistent presence, flexible and secure basing, and reach. Once again, it doesn't.

Finally, the QDR notes that a key foreign policy objective over the next decade will be shaping the strategic choices of countries like China.[11] It is not clear, however, on how the U.S. military can assist in pursuing this goal. Some analysts, dating back to the draft Defense Planning Guidance (DPG) of 1992, have contended that the United States could dissuade such states—or at least the rational ones—from attempting to compete with it by amassing vast military power and a sufficiently large technological edge to make such competition extremely expensive and highly unlikely to be successful—a theory both vague and overly optimistic when it comes to the ambitions of rising powers.[12] History suggests little reason to assume that the competition would be on U.S. terms and decided by our strategic logic.[13] But, whatever the merits of that strategy, it certainly will not be accomplished if America's competitors see an opposing military that is short on able bodies,[14] slow to reconstitute its warfighting capacity,[15] and not serious about meeting either the counterrevolution in military affairs or the challenges of expeditionary warfare—a critical component of projecting military power abroad.

Quo Vadis?

This brings us to the key question: What exactly do we want the role of the Marine Corps to be? In QDR discussions and internal debates at Marine Corps headquarters, this question, though muted, has been omnipresent. Recently, the debate has become public as well. Do we want the Corps to retain its investment in amphibious operations and its ability to inject a U.S. military presence forcibly at a time and place of our choice, or should it return to its pre–World War II mission and its rich legacy as a classical "small-wars" force?[16] The answer to this question will substantially shape the missions and investment portfolios of the Navy, and also have a corresponding ripple effect on the Army. Below I examine two scenarios—one which posits the Marine Corps of the twenty-first century as a forcible-entry force and the second as a small-wars force—and offer a "hybrid force" as a viable alternative.

A Forcible-Entry Marine Corps. Historian and columnist Max Boot recalls seeing a big demonstration of amphibious warfare at a marine base in North Carolina. "The demonstration was impressive," he writes. "All those amtracs, and hovercraft and landing ships—what a spectacle! Watching from the stands, I thought it was glorious but also an anachronism, like watching a cavalry charge in the 1930s."[17] Yet the reality remains that American interests are threatened in places like the Persian Gulf, the Indian Ocean, and the vast expanse of the Pacific.[18] These fundamentally maritime theaters include close friends and competitors, with long sea-lines of communication, vulnerable extended-basing systems, extended anti-access defenses that can be systemically attacked and rolled back, and key economic centers and overseas assets that can be put at risk by isolation or seizure. Any strategy that presumes to shape the behavior of states must have the military capability to make antagonists aware that these key sites can be placed at risk at a time and place of our choice. A Marine Corps that retains a formidable forcible-entry force is not a nostalgic reprise of *The Sands of Iwo Jima*. To the contrary, it reflects strategic realities as they appear today and are likely to exist in the future. We have not seen the end of the need to penetrate inland with robust forces in order to strike at an adversary's critical vulnerability or seize a key objective. The need to conduct power-projection operations from the sea, jointly with other forces, is both a viable and very necessary capability.

An objective assessment of the emerging security environment places a premium on the expeditionary capabilities the Navy/Marine Corps team brings to the table, including forcible entry from the sea. One can debate technological trend lines in military affairs and argue about the primacy of state or nonstate actors in our security agenda, but one cannot argue away the tyranny of geography. A number of possible future adversaries and many of our friends are found far from America's shores; the need to project power at great distances and to support allies and our own forces in sustained missions is not going away.[19]

Although it is true that we have not employed amphibious forces in an assault role since Inchon, the Marines have hardly been covered in cobwebs. Washington has used Marine amphibious forces for crisis response and military operations several times a year for some time now—roughly seventy-three times since 1983. Even discounting these operations, looking backward does not always produce the best set of guidelines for force-planning. We have not dropped a nuclear bomb for an even longer period of time, nor have we sunk any submarines since WWII, yet no one has proposed eliminating the strategic bomber fleet or the Navy's fleet of submarines. No one has so far launched a ballistic missile attack at the continental United States, and yet we are prepared to spend billions upon billions of dollars to field a national missile defense system. These investments are predicated upon what might need to be done to defend ourselves and their presumed influence on the strategic behavior of present and future adversaries.

Five distinct advantages accrue to the United States from possession of a robust amphibious power-projection capability:

- *It produces a credible deterrent.* The ability to conduct a powerful forcible-entry operation at a time and place of our choosing produces a credible deterrent against would-be aggressors. This deterrent holds an adversary at greater risk than do the often transitory effects of power-projection by strike or long-range precision fires because it threatens destruction of the regime or the seizure of something the adversary holds dear. Many "states of concern" have considerable coastal regions, with significant economic assets or basing facilities that could be placed at risk. The ability of the United States to isolate, seize, and hold these facilities can be a major factor in the internal deliberations of those countries.

- *It negates an adversary's anti-access strategy. Strategic success is often dependent on the ability to attack or undermine the opponent's strategy.* A number of states with interests inimical—or potentially inimical—to the United States are investing heavily in the ability to fend off U.S. power-projection forces. Washington's reluctance to modernize the amphibious fleet to deal with this strategy only increases the strategy's attractiveness and value. To the degree that we can avoid defensive systems and slice through or over littoral regions to seize key objectives directly, we negate our adversaries' investment in anti-access capabilities and reduce their confidence in being safe from a regime-threatening military threat.

- *It complicates a defender's strategy.* Our investment in power-projection, expeditionary forces, and littoral dominance compels our adversaries to invest in a host of surveillance and defensive systems. Conversely, if we did not pose the potential for decisive forcible-entry operations, future aggressors could invest more intensely in a narrower sphere. We should want an adversary to invest in securing the breadth and depth of his country against a powerful thrust from sea and air rather than being able to spend the money elsewhere. A government that is not concerned about a direct assault into its territory can, for example, invest heavily in surface-to-air systems to counter our air dominance and impose higher costs on attacking U.S. aviation forces. A country that is concerned about a direct assault, however, must split its resources and attention to counter attacks from both land and air. In short, maintaining a power-projection capability expands what an adversary must defend and dilutes his overall effectiveness relative to our capabilities.

- *It ensures access.* In the simplest terms, forcible-entry capabilities ensure access to particular areas for U.S. forces in times of crisis rather than leaving policymakers dependent on foreign governments to provide overflight rights or port and airfield access. We can, when necessary, inject credible combat power directly into the opposing state. Ultimately, U.S. interests should not be held hostage to hopes for cooperation or the whims of third-party states that may not share our interests at a given time. As we have seen in operations in Afghanistan and Saddam's Iraq, there are political dynamics at work that may constrain or completely eliminate American access during military interventions.

- *It ensures freedom of action.* A sea-based force is less reliant on permissions to overfly national airspaces or use transportation hubs and networks within sovereign states. The QDR specifically notes the need to enhance strategic and operational freedom of action by increasing the stealth, persistence, flexible basing, and strategic reach of American power.[20] If necessary it can stand poised in international waters as a support to diplomacy, without generating political costs for basing rights, or exposing U.S. forces to attack. A potent sea-based joint force does not require permission slips or lengthy and debilitating diplomatic negotiations before it assembles and moves on target; it can generate the freedom of action and reach explicitly required in the QDR.

All told, the strategic and operational advantages of sea-based forcible entry are clear and compelling. Forcible entry should be viewed not as a narrow, somewhat dated mission, but rather as giving the United States a distinctly asymmetric capability of its own in the future. Without these capabilities, the Navy and Marine Corps cannot provide Washington with the ability to respond immediately and credibly to challenges to America's security interests in far reaches of the world. With these capabilities, it can help shape the thinking and investments of potential adversaries and friends who live in the shadow of rising powers.

Given that the demand for power-projection in maritime theaters is rising, and that the inherent flexibility of expeditionary forces generates great utility for policymakers, the force structure of the Marine Corps should be expanded. At present, the Corps is undermanned due to efforts over the past few years to respond to new security dynamics. The Marines have added fleet antiterrorist security units and a chemical-biological incident response force, and have increased their contribution to joint activities. Over time, budgetary pressures due to rising recruiting, health-care, and personnel costs have further reduced the Corps below the force structure (three divisions, three air wings) mandated by Congress, and certainly below the level with which the Marines themselves are comfortable.[21] Management efficiencies and innovative manning approaches have reached their efficacy limit. Doing more with less only works up to a point. It is time to provide the Marines with more manpower to reestablish adequate personnel levels, increase the numbers in the education pipelines, and decrease the debilitating impact of today's high operational tempo.

A forcible-entry Marine Corps would need a minimum of three complete Marine divisions. This would necessitate a total of nine infantry regiments of twenty-seven infantry battalions—an increase of three battalions. A full complement of seven combat support battalions per division would be required, of which four would be artillery battalions, including one high mobility artillery rocket system (HIMARS) battalion to provide deep, area fires. The other three would consist of a reconnaissance battalion, tank battalion, and amphibious assault battalion. The Marine Corps end strength would have to be increased from today's temporary level of 180,000 to an authorization of roughly 195,000 to fulfill this plan.

The Marines would also need to acquire more than 1,000 expeditionary fighting vehicles (EFVs)—the program's targeted number. The EFV has been the Corps's number one ground acquisition program for more than a decade, replacing the aging assault amphibious vehicle (AAV) that has been in service since 1972. The EFV will provide Marine assault elements with better operational and tactical mobility, both in the water and ashore. Designed to launch from ships stationed over the horizon, it will travel at speeds in excess of twenty nautical miles per hour and provide greater maneuverability and speed ashore. The speed and protective design of the EFV will reduce the vulnerability of assault forces to enemy threats at sea and on land. Once ashore, an EFV will provide Marines with an armored personnel carrier with communications and navigation gear improved over that of the existing Vietnam-era amphibious tractor, as well as advanced armor and nuclear, biological, and chemical protection. In addition to reducing the vulnerability of the Marines on board, the EFV will have a 30mm gun, a substantial upgrade in fire support. Altogether, the new capabilities of the EFV will significantly enhance the lethality and survivability of Marine maneuver units.

Likewise, current Marine aviation plans would have to be modified. The existing aviation strategy is a well-designed effort to enhance support to Marines over a wide range of missions.[22] To support a forcible-entry mission, however, three more Joint Strike Fighter squadrons will need to be added to the current programmed level. In addition, the Marines will need to enhance their unmanned aerial vehicle assets (UAVs), a capability the Corps has been slow to exploit as fully as it should. Finally, the V-22 tilt-rotor Osprey should remain a key component of the aviation-combat element of any forcible-entry Marine expeditionary force, resulting in a full program-buy of 420 aircraft in eighteen squadrons. At a distance of 110 nautical miles, a squadron of MV-22s is capable of lifting a 975-man Marine battalion in four waves in under four hours. This contrasts greatly with nine waves of CH-46s accomplishing the same mission in eighteen hours. The greater range and speed of the MV-22 will significantly increase the operational reach of assault forces and expand the battle space an opponent must defend. In addition to further diluting the enemy's defenses, the increased speed and reach of this aircraft will reduce the time required to build up our own forces, minimize vulnerability during the insertion phase, and sharply enhance the operational tempo of a joint force.

A Small-Wars Marine Corps. Some, such as the aforementioned historian Max Boot, have suggested that the Marine Corps revert to its pre–World War II roots.[23] Boot would like to see the Corps focus on America's existing threat, exploit its impressive versatility, and return to its small-wars legacy:

> Re-embracing that role is an urgent task because the future of warfare is looking more and more like the Marines' past. "Small wars"—encompassing counterinsurgency, nation-building, and peacekeeping—seem likely to be the major challenge for the U.S. as it fights the war on terror. The Marines are well-placed to play a

leading role in this kind of irregular conflict, but to do so they will have to leave their glorious World War II heritage even further behind.[24]

This school of thought has its proponents within the Marine Corps as well. They argue that state-based conventional warfare is an unlikely contingency, and that the migration of conventional threats into a mosaic of irregular challengers and terrorists employing weapons of mass destruction requires a unique response. Certainly, advocates of a small-wars Marine Corps have a point. Even the QDR recognizes this shift: "In the post-September 11 world, irregular warfare has emerged as the dominant form of warfare confronting the United States."[25] And although a more traditional form of warfare has not disappeared, today's pressing reality requires us to focus on how best to deal with this irregular form and adapt to its characteristics.[26]

But while the Pentagon recognizes the threat this kind of irregular warfare poses, the Office of the Secretary of Defense appears fixated on the Operation Enduring Freedom model—using special operations forces and CIA operatives—as the most desirable form of executing interventions in ungoverned areas. As we have seen in both Afghanistan and Iraq, however, there are limits to what a mix of SOF and CIA can do with indigenous partners. Moreover, not all of the problems we face in Afghanistan and Iraq can be overcome with U.S. training or technology. Fighting these fights still requires highly trained, well-led, professional ground forces.[27]

The future promises a more diverse set of challengers, wielding an array of tools and evolving stratagems. In some respects, the past presented a more comforting threat, one we were mentally and physically prepared to address. The scale of the threat in the Cold War was daunting, but it was somewhat predictable, with its order of battle and approach to warfare laid out in templates. Tomorrow's threat is more protean and constantly evolving, requiring on our part a capacity to learn continuously and adapt. One can see this emerging trend in this past summer's clash in southern Lebanon. The amorphous Hezbollah carefully trained its forces based on its understanding of Israeli tactics. They prepared highly disciplined, well-trained, distributed cells to contest the Israeli Defense Forces, mixing guerrilla tactics and technology in densely packed urban centers. Their tenacity and sophistication were a surprise to veteran Israeli paratroopers.

The most common characteristic of future threats will be their diversity. Their structure and operating style will not be readily reduced to a simple template. They will exploit the modern technologies of a global economy, present us with asymmetric modes of operation, and continually surprise us with unanticipated tactics. They will not remain static or subject to predictive analysis.[28] In an age of "adaptive asymmetry," the contest will be one of Darwinian Davids and Goliaths, where slingshots and stones deliver just the opening shots, and survival depends on being both the fittest and most adaptive actor in the battle space.[29]

Future opponents will avoid fighting the American way of war—in which we optimize our material and information-age dominance—and will not abide by our preferred rules. Indeed, our opponents appear to accept no rules of war. We will face primitive forms of warfare and criminal activity that long ago were proscribed by Western society. We can also expect to see a lot of tactical aping, with our opponent learning from us and discovering how to use high technology in unique and unanticipated ways. Future enemies will seek their own degree of "shock and awe" with barbarity rather than precision weaponry. Arguably, the Marine Corps could extend its well-founded legacy of institutional agility to address this new era of warfighting.

Another reason to look toward the Marine Corps in the small-war arena is the likely rise in urban conflicts, an area where the Marines are recognized as experts.[30] The American military currently enjoys almost complete dominance in the global commons, particularly at sea and in space. Our command of the global commons translates into an unparalleled capacity to leverage the oceans, space, and airpower more than any other country. That said, it is well understood by those opposing modern, technologically advanced, Western military forces that complex terrain affords defenders a number of advantages that tend to offset or at least substantially mitigate the conventional superiority of such forces. Recent combat operations suggest a shift toward these more complex contested zones.[31]

These zones include the dense urban jungles and the congested littorals where the majority of the world's population and economic activity is centered. They remain the most likely employment area for U.S. expeditionary forces and the most likely environment in which U.S. forces will be engaged in irregular combat. As seen in Kosovo, Afghanistan, Iraq, and, most recently, Lebanon, irregular adversaries are adopting tactics and modes of operations to offset our technological advantages in intelligence collection, surveillance, and reconnaissance. The engagement of American forces in these areas through a range of effective asymmetric tactics is intended to protract conflicts, increase their costs, and, ultimately, sap American will.

The complex terrain of the world's urban centers will likely be the insurgent's and terrorist's jungle of the twenty-first century.[32] Urban terrain, with its dense population, transportation networks, public services, and infrastructure provides a safe haven to the urban guerrilla, with multiple avenues of escape and the ability to hide while planning and rehearsing operations. The density of the urban complex provides sufficient cover and noise to mask the adversary's preparation and attack position. The decades-long trend toward urbanization will not abate; it will lead, rather, to continued social instability and potential challenges to political control and public security.[33] To secure our interests in today's deadly and dynamic security context, we must master the ambiguity and chaos of these contested zones.

A commitment by the Corps to handling the twenty-first-century version of the small-wars problem would require alterations in the Corps's basic structure. The basic Marine air-ground task force would need to be retrained, and it might be better organized into more modular Marine-brigade-sized components, not unlike the reorganization taking place in the Army.[34] Ground units may be further adapted to provide specific expertise. One option would be to retain thirty infantry battalions, but divide them into fifteen regular infantry battalions and fifteen Raider battalions. The regular battalions, augmented with light armor assets, would be tasked with securing large areas and becoming masters of urban warfare, with frequent opportunities to train in this operational environment. The Raiders would form a more specialized unit, which would regularly rotate into the Marine Component at U.S. Special Operations Command. Instead of having heavy assets like tanks, long-range rocket systems, and amphibious assault craft, the Marines would be substantially lighter and more mobile. Plans for replacements for their M1A1 main battle tanks and the EFV would be scrapped. The EFV, which costs $12 million and is optimized for rare ship-to-shore maneuver, is ideal for a forcible-entry Marine Corps. It is, however, inadequate for tactical maneuver during small wars.[35] A new light-armored vehicle (LAV) program would have to be initiated; something between the existing LAV and the German Puma would be optimal.

To be capable of dealing with today's small wars, the Marine Corps would also need to create new units to address specific capability shortfalls. They would include information-warfare battalions to upgrade the Corps's psychological operations capability, security cooperation units, civil affairs battalions, and military police assets. Additional units for chemical-biological incident response would also be needed. Such capabilities are much more relevant for tomorrow's "savage wars of peace." Manpower from artillery units could be used as offsets for some of these additional requirements. Other capabilities, including intelligence assets like human exploitation teams and analysts, would remain at the same overall level, but would be decentralized to work within tactical units at the regimental and battalion levels to increase those organizations' depth for 24/7 operations. Recent operational experience highlights the increase in actionable intelligence at lower levels of counterinsurgency and stabilization operations.[36]

Reorienting the Marines for complex irregular wars would require a somewhat different aviation-combat element as well. The most significant difference would be sharply reduced buys of the MV-22 Osprey. At somewhere between $75 million and $80 million apiece, the tilt-rotor Osprey is not the right aircraft for countering insurgencies in the developing world. The complexity of this hybrid machine, half-aircraft and half-helicopter, does not bring desirable operational characteristics to the table at an acceptable price. Its reach and speed, though significant, are not usually needed in small wars. Since its speed and self-deployability make the Osprey a superb platform for special operations, some may, in fact, be needed, but the aviation component devoted to Special Operations Command would be the only Marine unit to employ this aircraft. The Marines would rely upon some other traditional, and much more affordable, medium-lift helicopter for their everyday needs.[37]

Small wars are culture-centric and require highly trained units with special regional and foreign-area expertise. Because the training and education pipeline required to provide the necessary intellectual agility, culture, and language skills is so much longer, a larger end strength would be required. Furthermore, the need to feed qualified Marines into SOCOM would certainly increase the demand for additive end strength as well. Thus, active-duty end strength of 190,000–195,000 Marines is recommended for a small-wars Corps devoted to addressing the increasingly challenging nature of complex irregular warfare.

The Future: A Hybrid Marine Corps. So what exactly is the future of today's American Spartans? This question gives rise to a great many others: Should the Corps be optimized for its traditional role as the country's potent amphibious sword? Does the United States really want and need the capacity to maneuver seamlessly from theater to theater and penetrate an enemy's territorial defenses in a decisive manner? Has a lack of strategic vision, an over-reliance on precision targeting, and a misperception of the versatility of amphibious forces culminated in a decision not to fund or plan adequately for retaining this capability? How can the United States create a modern force that will achieve the sort of cost shifts for adversaries suggested by the QDR? How else can we generate a cost-imposing strategy that forces an adversary to have to secure the breadth and depth of his own country against a powerful thrust from the world's foremost maritime power? Would not a diminution of our once formidable assault ability allow future opponents to narrow their defensive investments and thwart a one-dimensional American attack? How does this shape the behavior of future states of concern? And, finally, how is this capability to be maintained—and with it the operational freedom apparently desired by the E-ring of the Pentagon—if the Navy's ship-building plan does not provide the vessels needed to carry it out?

For the foreseeable future, the United States faces a world in which most of our adversaries will resort to irregular warfare to confound our global goals.[38] And while the most recent QDR recognizes that as a fact of life, it underestimates what sort of military America will need to handle it. Irregular warfare does not reduce the need for boots on the ground; in many scenarios—urban warfare or postconflict pacification, for example—it requires more, as well as more small-unit, highly skilled infantrymen than any imaginable number of special operations forces or CIA operatives could ever provide. If the United States is serious about fighting this kind of warfare, how can it ignore the obvious need to increase the land forces required to meet the challenge successfully?

As the above analysis suggests, a simplistic choice of a big, power-projecting Marine Corps versus a Corps focused on the small-wars mission is flawed—and dangerous. Given America's global goals, its multifaceted responsibilities, and the potential adversaries it faces, it must have the capacity to carry out both military tasks effectively.

As history has shown repeatedly, no country—especially one like the United States, whose interests span every continent—can predict exactly what threats it will face in the future. While irregular warfare is our current worry, there is no guarantee that it will supplant the state-based and conventional threats we have known in the past. Many who have made similar assumptions about the future have been proved badly mistaken. State-based conflict is less likely than it once was, but it is certainly not extinct. And, indeed, the less pre-pared we are for that kind of conflict, the more likely our adversaries will see it as an opportunity to be exploited.

Nor should we assume all state-centric warfare will be completely conventional. Tomorrow's conflicts may involve a fusion of tactics that defy the black and white classification of either conventional or irregular warfare. In fact, some of today's best thinking acknowledges the blurring of lines between modes of war.[39] Rather than the simplistic quad chart found in the new National Defense Strategy, future scenarios will present unique combinational or hybrid threats specifically designed to target U.S. vulnerabilities. Conventional, irregular, and catastrophic terrorist challenges will not be distinct styles; they may well all be present in some form. States may blend high-tech capabilities, such as antisatellite weapons, with terrorism and cyberwarfare directed against financial targets. Similarly, as we have learned in recent years, states will not have a monopoly on violence. We could face major states capable of supporting covert and indirect means of attack, as well as super-empowered fanatics capable of direct and highly lethal attacks undercutting the global order. In short, opponents will be capable of what Marine Lieutenant General James Mattis has called "Hybrid Wars."[40]

Hybrid wars do not allow us the luxury of building single-mission forces. It is clear that the United States needs both a capable forcible-entry force and a force that can competently address the increasingly lethal irregular adversary. Because of their institutional capacity for excellence and continuous evolution and tactical improvisation, the Marines are well suited for this admittedly difficult task; they have the doctrinal basis to excel in hybrid conflict.[41]

The resulting hybrid force structure is a configuration that blends the tasks of forcible entry and irregular warfare (see table 5-1 on page 133). Like all hybrids, this design contains compromises that offer greater flexibility at the expense of specialization or optimized capabilities for very narrow functions. It is more manpower-intensive than today's force and will require substantially enhanced training programs to ensure that ground units are fully prepared to respond to a broad range of missions. Rather than having specialized infantry units for amphibious, urban, or counterinsurgency tasks, it relies upon traditional Marine rifle battalions to serve as modular expeditionary units, able to respond appropriately across a broad range of missions—an appealing prospect in uncertain times. The Marines field more light-armored vehicles than EFVs to enhance their ground tactical mobility, and enough amphibious vehicles are retained to be capable of conducting forcible-entry operations. The role of organic fire support is altered, however. Marine artillery is reshaped to emphasize the flexibility and accuracy of the 120mm mortar, with some 155mm artillery for general support. The hybrid force also has more intelligence and information-warfare capability than today's current Marine Corps. The Marines make a larger contribution to SOCOM in the form of an additional Marine battalion and an additional foreign military training unit (FMTU).

As table 5-1 indicates, the hybrid force's aviation component would be roughly similar to the current Marine aviation strategy and programmed force. The Marines would complete their planned acquisition of V-22s as planned, but also increase their heavy-lift helicopter force. Unmanned systems would be enhanced and a new system—an armed, long-loiter UAV, which would provide responsive, all-weather support and serve as a company commander's personal fire support system—would be included in the proposed force.

In addition to being properly sized, the hybrid force would also be equipped and sustained for global operations. The global war on terror has made extraordinary demands on Marine Corps equipment, particularly ground combat gear and combat service support equipment. The need for additional gear for units involved in extended counterinsurgency efforts has required modifications to unit tables of equipment, particularly for communications, force protection, and convoy security. Extended operations in Iraq, Afghanistan, and elsewhere over the past several years have severely tested materiel readiness and the ability of the depots to sustain Marine forces for myriad missions around the globe. Because of extensive vehicle use and adverse conditions, in just a few years the Marines' combat gear has been subject to the equivalent of its expected lifetime's worth of degradation. All the services have this same problem—the need to "reset" the material readiness of each armed force. This discussion deals only with the Corps's existing equipment and does not begin to address modernization plans.

The Marine Corps commandant testified last year that roughly $12 billion in ground and aviation "reset" requirements had been

TABLE 5-1
ALTERNATIVE MARINE FORCE STRUCTURES

	Current	Forcible-Entry Marine Corps	Small-Wars Marine Corps	Hybrid Force
Ground Combat				
Infantry Battalions	24	27	15	27
Reconnaissance Battalions	2	3	—	3
Raider Battalions	2	—	15	3[c]
Tank Battalions	2.3	3	0	0
Assault Amphibian Vehicle Battalions	2	3	0	2
Light Armored Vehicle Battalions	3	3	6	6
Artillery Battalions	10	12[a]	6[b]	9[b]/3
Civil Affairs Battalions	0	0	2	1
Engineer Battalions	2	3	3	3
Information Warfare Battalions	0	0	2	1
Intelligence Battalions	2	3	0	3
Foreign Military Training Units	2	0	3	3[c]
Marine Aviation				
Fighter/Attack Squadrons	12/7	18 (JSF)	9 (JSF)	15 (JSF)
Rotary Wing Squadrons				
Light Helicopter Squadrons	6	3	6	6
Medium Helicopter Squadrons	14	18 (V-22)	15 (S-92)/3CV-22[c]	15 (V-22)
Heavy Helicopter Squadrons	9	9	6	9
Unmanned Aerial Vehicle Squadrons	2	3	3	3
Armed Long Loiter UAV Units	0	—	—	2
End Strength	**175**	**195**	**195**	**190–95**

SOURCE: Author's calculations.
NOTES: a. Lightweight 155mm batteries; b.120mm mortar batteries; c. Assigned to MarSoC, SOCOM.

identified.[42] This shortfall is in addition to the Corps's annual operating costs associated with Operation Iraqi Freedom/Operation Enduring Freedom (OIF/OEF). Over the past year, internal reports have suggested that the reset estimate is outdated and low, with the total unfunded acquisition shortfall now closer to $16 billion and growing each year. Thus, significantly increased supplemental funding is essential if the Marines are to dig themselves out of the current hole.

Historically, the annual figure for Marine Corps procurement averages under $1.5 billion in constant dollars.[43] If required to absorb the entire $16 billion cost to reset itself within the current annual budget procurement allocation, it will take more than a decade for the Corps to recover, and it will come at the price of deferring all Marine modernization programs for that decade.

Congress has been generous with supplemental budgets, but these resources have not kept pace with ongoing combat losses and the excessive wear and tear that the Leathernecks have been putting on their vehicles and weapons in two separate conflicts. While the Pentagon's plans are to increase funding for Marine acquisition programs, additional funding will be needed. In addition to the $16 billion for reset, an annual procurement budget of $3 billion is needed.[44]

Conclusion

The 2006 QDR should have been favorable to the Marines, given the inherent hybrid capacities of the Corps. Instead, it failed to recognize the full potential of the Corps in irregular warfare and ignored the power-projection capability of a modernized amphibious force acting jointly with the other services. In place of a powerful, hybrid force, we have a Marine Corps that is inade-quate for handling both missions. The Office of the Secretary of Defense is trying to fit the Corps into a special operations forces shoe that doesn't fit and hoping against history and geography that the country will never face a requirement to land substantial numbers of conventional forces against a defended coast. The result is an underfunded and underutilized Marine Corps.

Potentially, the country already possesses the ability to conduct both forcible entry and persistent global engagement in irregular conflict with one expeditionary force package. A robust and modernized Marine Corps is the solution. The Marines have the ability to close rapidly, employ decisively, and sustain effectively forces from the sea. They can also respond to requirements as they emerge from the global war on terror and carry out peace support missions within contested zones. Adequately manned, properly trained and equipped, the Marine Corps can provide the nation and its leaders with the kind of hybrid force capable of making the transition between sea and shore, between regular and irregular forces, and between warfighting and reconstruction tasks—today's most demanding mission profiles. It could, as outlined above, serve two major expeditionary missions. In today's wars and those we might face in the future, such a hybrid force is the most cost-effective solution.

It might be useful to recall that the ancient Spartans never did best their Athenian opponents with their superior land power. For years the Spartans stuck to their strengths as a ground force. But a one-dimensional capability proved insufficient against a thinking opponent, as Victor Davis Hanson has shown.[45] It was not until the Spartans created their own navy and naval infantry and began to apply diplomacy and information operations that they were able to create the conditions for victory. They learned, in short, that they could not be uncontested experts at just one form of warfare and still assure success. Belatedly, but ultimately successfully, they became a hybrid force. There is a lesson here for those who expect America's Spartans to excel tomorrow as well as they have in the past.

Appendix

The essays in this book have asserted that numbers matter—that, as Stalin famously observed, "Quantity has a quality all its own." The charts in this appendix measure the current troubles of the U.S. military in stark terms: a long decline in weapons spending, as well as a deep reduction in personnel levels. But they also indirectly measure a change in American society and government: As the country grows wealthier, it seems less willing to devote a sufficient slice of its gross domestic product to its defense. Conversely, we spend an increasing amount on entitlements; if spending levels are a reflection of priorities, Social Security has supplanted national security as the government's primary purpose.

Tables 1 and 2 and figures 1 and 4 paint a broad-brush picture of a "decapitalization" of U.S. armed forces—the result of the post–Cold War "peace dividend." Table 1 tracks the decline in overall defense spending, a remarkably symmetrical trough beginning in 1990, bottoming out at a level almost $100 billion per year lower in 1998, and only lately achieving a return to the 1990 level—but only when emergency spending for Iraq and Afghanistan are factored in. Table 2, focused on procurement, shows the true trend more clearly: Weapons modernization spending has never returned to the level of 1990 (and there is no plan to achieve that level of spending again). Figure 4 takes an even broader look, graphically portraying the "procurement holiday" that began in the second term of Ronald Reagan and leaves defense procurement today at less than two-thirds of that peak. Finally, figure 1 shows how the procurement patterns of the Clinton years stacked up against the requirements set by the Joint Staff and estimated by the

Congressional Budget Office, again indicating a level of spending about two-thirds of that needed.

Table 3 tracks the continued decline of an "all-volunteer" force too small to meet its mission. From a total active strength of nearly 2.1 million, U.S. forces quickly fell below 1.4 million by the late 1990s, and they remain at about 1.35 million, despite the demands of more than five years of extended combat. Figure 5 reveals that, at the same time, the cost of each troop has steadily risen to more than one and a half times that of what it was when the all-volunteer force was created. Figure 6 also shows how the cost of equipping and training a professional force has grown dramatically, roughly tripling over the period of the volunteer force.

Figures 2, 3, and 7 outline what is perhaps the saddest trend of all: a richer America less willing to sacrifice for the purposes of national defense. Figure 2 reveals that the amount of GDP devoted to defense spending has shrunk from the levels of Vietnam to the late Cold War to the post–9/11 period—from 10 percent of our wealth to 6 or 7 percent to less than 4 percent, respectively. Figure 3 indicates levels of defense spending during a number of American conflicts and crises. It shows the post–9/11 level almost indistinguishable from the "peace dividend" period of the 1990s, and a paltry effort in comparison to those of previous wars. Finally, figure 7 tracks year-by-year spending since 1990, highlighting the administration's intent during what it describes as "the Long War" to continue a low level of military spending and, indeed, to make deeper reductions.

FIGURE 1
CLINTON PROCUREMENT DEFICIT (1992–2001)
IN CURRENT U.S. DOLLARS (MILLIONS)

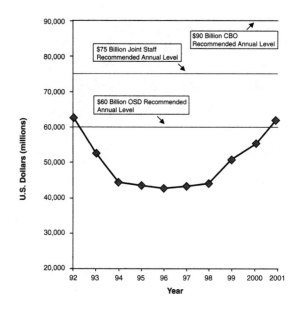

SOURCE: Adapted from "Trends in U.S. Defense Spending, Procurement, and Readiness: The Growing Gap Between Strategy, Force Plans, and Resources," Anthony H. Cordesman, Center for Strategic and International Studies, Washington, D.C., April 1998, p. 34.

FIGURE 2

FEDERAL OUTLAYS BY MAJOR CATEGORY, PERCENTAGE OF GDP,
FY1962–FY2010

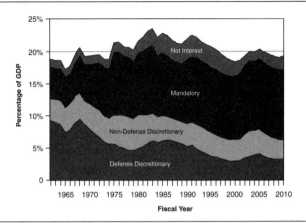

SOURCE: Stephen Daggett, "Defense Budget: Long-Term Challenges for FY2006 and Beyond," *CRS Report for Congress*, April 20, 2006, figure 3, p. 4.

FIGURE 3

NATIONAL DEFENSE SPENDING AS A PERCENT OF GNP IN PREVIOUS CONFLICTS AND CRISES (TOTAL FEDERAL OUTLAYS)

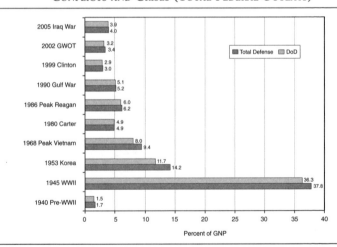

SOURCE: Adapted from Office of the Under Secretary of Defense (Comptroller), *National Defense Budget Estimates for FY2007*, Washington, Department of Defense, March 2006, table 7-7 pp. 216–217. Budget total is for entire national defense, not just the Department of Defense.

FIGURE 4

PROCUREMENT VERSUS STEADY STATE LEVELS
UNDER DOD'S CURRENT PLAN

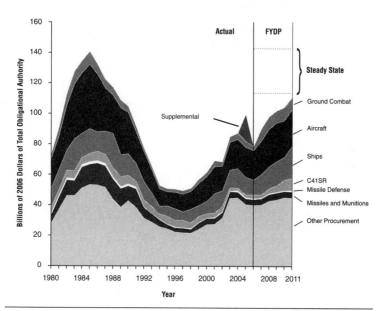

SOURCE: Adapted from *The Long-Term Implications of Current Defense Plans and Alternatives: Detailed Update for FY2006*, Congressional Budget Office, January 2006, figure 3-31a, p. 76.

FIGURE 5

MILITARY PERSONNEL BUDGET AUTHORITY PER ACTIVE DUTY
TROOP INDEXED TO FY1972

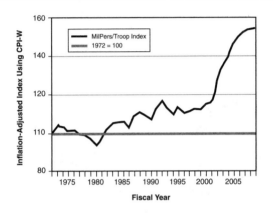

SOURCE: Stephen Daggett, "Defense Budget: Long-Term Challenges for FY2006 and
Beyond," *CRS Report for Congress*, April 20, 2006, figure 5, p. 8.

FIGURE 6

OPERATION AND MAINTENANCE BUDGET AUTHORITY PER
ACTIVE DUTY TROOP FY1955–FY2010

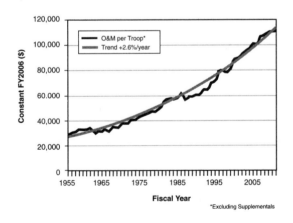

SOURCE: Stephen Daggett, "Defense Budget: Long-Term Challenges for FY2006 and
Beyond," *CRS Report for Congress*, April 20, 2006, figure 6, p. 9.

FIGURE 7

NATIONAL DEFENSE SPENDING OUTLAYS AS A PERCENTAGE OF GDP
FY1990–2011 (BY FISCAL YEAR)

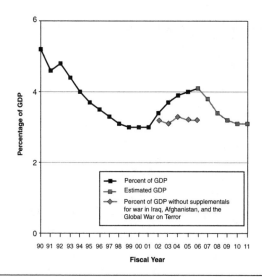

SOURCE: Data from Historical Tables, *Budget of the United States Government*, Fiscal Year 2007,
U.S. Government Printing Office, Washington, D.C., February 2006, pp. 24, 53–54.

TABLE 1

NATIONAL DEFENSE BUDGET AUTHORITY FY1990–2011
(BY FISCAL YEAR IN BILLIONS OF DOLLARS)

Fiscal Year	Current Dollars	Fiscal Year 2007 Dollars
1990	303.3	452.7
1991	288.9	428.6
1992	295.1	405.9
1993	281.1	402.9
1994	263.3	369.5
1995	266.4	366.1
1996	266.2	358.0
1997	270.4	355.6
1998	271.3	348.0
1999	292.3	365.7
2000	304.1	370.9
2001	334.9	396.8
2002	362.1	418.0
2003	456.2	511.6
2004	490.6	533.9
2005	505.8	533.1
2006	491.8	503.7
2007	463.0	463.0
2008	485.2	473.5
2009	505.3	481.4
2010	515.3	479.1
2011	526.1	477.2

SOURCE: Historical Tables, *Budget of the United States Government*, Fiscal Year 2007, U.S. Government Printing Office, Washington, D.C., February 2006, pp. 86–89.

TABLE 2
NATIONAL DEFENSE BUDGET AUTHORITY FOR PROCUREMENT
(BY FISCAL YEAR IN MILLIONS OF DOLLARS)

Fiscal Year	Current Dollars	Fiscal Year 2007 Dollars
1990	81.4	111.3
1991	71.7	N/A
1992	63.0	N/A
1993	52.8	67.0
1994	44.1	55.0
1995	43.6	53.5
1996	42.6	51.4
1997	43.0	51.2
1998	44.8	53.0
1999	51.1	59.6
2000	55.0	63.1
2001	62.6	71.0
2002	62.7	70.1
2003	78.5	86.1
2004	83.1	89.0
2005	96.6	101.0
2006	86.2	88.1
2007	84.2	84.2
2008	99.8	97.7
2009	108.6	104.1
2010	111.7	104.9
2011	117.7	108.2

SOURCE: Historical Tables, *Budget of the United States Government*, Fiscal Year 2007, U.S Government Printing Office, Washington D.C., February 2006, pp.86–89; Office of the Under Secretary of Defense (Comptroller), *National Defense Budget Estimates for FY2007*, Washington, D.C., Department of Defense, March 2006.

TABLE 3
DEPARTMENT OF DEFENSE MANPOWER FY 1990–2007
(END STRENGTH IN THOUSANDS)

Fiscal Year	Army	Navy	Marine Corps	Air Force	Total End Strength
1990	751	583	197	539	2,070
1991	725	571	195	511	2,002
1992	611	542	185	470	1,808
1993	572	510	178	444	1,704
1994	541	469	174	426	1,610
1995	509	435	174	400	1,518
1996	491	417	175	389	1,472
1997	492	396	174	378	1,440
1998	484	382	173	367	1,406
1999	479	373	173	361	1,386
2000	482	373	173	356	1,384
2001	481	378	173	354	1,386
2002	487	383	174	368	1,412
2003	499	382	178	375	1,434
2004	500	373	178	377	1,428
2005	492	362	180	352	1,386
2006	482	353	175	352	1,362
2007	512	341	180	334	1,367

SOURCE: *National Defense Budget Estimates for FY 2007*, Office of the Under Secretary of Defense (Comptroller), March 2006.

Notes

Chapter 1: Numbers Matter

1. Theodore Roosevelt, *Citizenship, Politics, and the Elemental Virtues* (New York: Charles Scribner's Sons, 1925), 272.

2. See Harold and Margaret Sprout, *The Rise of American Naval Power: 1776–1918* (Princeton, N.J.: Princeton University Press), 1939.

3. "DOD Releases QDR to Chart Way Ahead to Confront Future," American Forces Information Service, February 3, 2006.

4. Bob Woodward, *The Commanders* (New York: Simon & Schuster, 1990).

5. Francis Fukuyama, "The End of History," *National Interest*, Summer 1989.

6. See Eliot Cohen, "The Mystique of U.S. Air Power," *Foreign Affairs* 73, no. 1 (January/February 1994): 109–24.

7. Vin Weber, "Tactical Retreat: Bill Clinton's Defense Budget," *National Review*, May 10, 1993.

8. Les Aspin, "Report of the Bottom-Up Review," Federation of American Scientists, http://www.fas.org/man/docs/bur/index.html (accessed October 30, 2006).

9. *National Defense Authorization Act for Fiscal Year 1997*, Public Law 104–201, 104th Congress (September 23, 1996), www.dod.mil/dodgc/olc/docs/1997NDAA.pdf (accessed November 14, 2006).

10. U.S. Department of Defense, *Report of the Quadrennial Defense Review*, May 1997, http://www.defenselink.mil/pubs/qdr (accessed October 30, 2006); see sections "The Secretary's Message" and "Section IV: Alternative Defense Postures." For additional analysis, see Michael Vickers and Steven Kosiak, *The Quadrennial Defense Review: An Assessment*, Center for Strategic and Budgetary Assessments, 1997, http://www.csbaonline.org (accessed October 30, 2006).

11. National Defense Panel, *Transforming Defense: National Security in the 21st Century*, 1997, 15, http://www.dtic.mil/ndp/FullDoc2.pdf (accessed November 14, 2006).

12. Ibid., 37.

13. William Cohen (U.S. Secretary of Defense) to Floyd Spence, (chairman of the U.S. House Armed Services Committee), December 17, 1997, www.dau.mil/pubs/pm/pmpdf98/ndpr-jf.pdf (accessed October 30, 2006).

14. See, for example, Hubert Vedrine, "The View from France's Foreign Minister," *Business Week Online*, January 29, 2001, http://www.businessweek.com/2001/01_05/b3717011.htm (accessed October 30, 2006).

15. See Anthony H. Cordesman, *Trends in U.S. Defense Spending: The Size of Funding, Procurement and Readiness Problems,* Center for Strategic and International Studies, October 9, 2000, 2, http://www.csis.org/media/csis /pubs/trendsusdefense%5B1%5D.pdf (accessed October 30, 2006).

16. James Mann, *Rise of the Vulcans: the History of Bush's War Cabinet* (New York: Viking Penguin, 2004).

17. George W. Bush, "A Distinctly American Internationalism" (speech, Ronald Reagan Presidential Library, Simi Valley, California, November 19, 1999), quoted in Bush for President, Inc., "Governor Bush Discusses Foreign Policy In Speech At Ronald Reagan Library," press release, http://www.fas.org/news/usa/1999/11/pr111999_nn.htm (accessed October 30, 2006).

18. George W. Bush, "A Period of Consequences" (speech, the Citadel, South Carolina, September 23, 1999), Citadel News Service, press release, September 23, 1999, http://pao.citadel.edu/pres_bush (accessed October 30, 2006).

19. Floyd D. Spence, "The Fiscal Year 2001 Defense Budget," *National Security Report* 4, no. 1 (February 2000): 2.

20. Dick Cheney (speech, Philadelphia, Pa., Republican National Convention, August 2, 2000), http://www.cbsnews.com/stories/2000/08/02/politics/main221310.shtml (accessed November 14, 2006).

21. CNN.com, "Special Event: Bush Nominates Donald Rumsfeld as Secretary of Defense," transcript of press conference aired December 28, 2000, http://transcripts.cnn.com/TRANSCRIPTS/0012/28/se.02.html (accessed October 30, 2006).

22. Ibid. Much of Rumsfeld's thinking about the technological nature of military transformation had been shaped by his service as chairman of two blue-ribbon panels, one on ballistic missile threats and a second on the role of space in national security issues. The ballistic missile report concluded that "the threat to the [United States] posed by these emerging [ballistic missile] capabilities is broader, more mature and evolving more rapidly than has been reported in estimates and reports by the Intelligence Community"; Commission to Assess the Ballistic Missile Threat to the United States,

"Report of the Commission to Assess the Ballistic Missile Threat to the United States," Federation of American Scientists, July 15, 1998, executive summary, http://www.fas.org/irp/threat/missile/rumsfeld/index.html (accessed October 30, 2006). The report accomplished the goal of its congressional sponsors: to create the basis for revived efforts and spending on national missile defense programs. The space commission served a similar purpose and reached similar kinds of conclusions: Advocates for national missile defenses argued that an effective system would be largely based in space. Thus, the commission found that it was in the "U.S. national interests to . . . develop and deploy the means to deter and defend against hostile acts directed at U.S. space assets and against the uses of space hostile to U.S. interests"; U.S. Department of Defense, "Report of the Commission to Assess United States National Security Space Management and Organization," January 11, 2001, http://www.defenselink.mil/pubs/space20010111.html (accessed October 30, 2006).

23. Mike Ferullo, "Bush Meets with Defense Leaders," CNN.com, January 10, 2001; Gary Schmitt and Tom Donnelly, "Spend More on Defense— Now," *Weekly Standard*, January 22, 2001, 25.

24. U.S. Department of Defense, *Quadrennial Defense Review Report*, September 2001, iii, http://www.defenselink.mil/pubs/qdr2001.pdf# search=%222001%20QDR%22 (accessed October 30, 2006).

25. Ibid, v.

26. Ibid, 17–22.

27. Author interview with Lieutenant General David Barno, January 2005.

28. George W. Bush, "President Delivers State of the Union Address" (speech, Washington, D.C., The White House, Office of the Press Secretary, January 29, 2002), http://www.whitehouse.gov/news/releases/2002/01/ 20020129-11.html (accessed November 14, 2006).

29. George W. Bush, *The 2002 National Security Strategy of the United States* (Washington, D.C.: The White House, September 2002), 7, http://www. whitehouse.gov/nsc/nss.pdf (accessed November 14, 2006).

30. George W. Bush, "President's Remarks to the Nation" (speech, Washington, D.C., The White House, Office of the Press Secretary, September 11, 2002), http://www.whitehouse.gov/news/releases/2002/09/ 20020911-3.html (accessed November 14, 2006).

31. Andrew Krepinevich, *Operation Iraqi Freedom: A First-Blush Assessment* (Washington, D.C.: Center for Strategic and Budgetary Assessments, 2003), i.

32. Donald Rumsfeld, "Secretary Rumsfeld Town Hall Meeting," Camp Buehring, Kuwait, December 8, 2004, http://www.defenselink.mil/ transcripts/2004/tr20041208-secdef1761.html (accessed November 14, 2006).

33. The Bush administration has chosen to meet the personnel demands of extended occupation duties in Iraq and Afghanistan by relying far more heavily on reserve component forces than in previous years while restricting growth of the active-duty Army and continuing to reduce the size of the other services, including the Marine Corps. Through the 1990s, reservists totaled about 12.5 million "man-days" of duty annually, whereas by 2003 the total had jumped to 63 million "man-days" and has remained at similarly high levels; see Christine E. Wormuth, *The Future of the National Guard and Reserves* (Washington, D.C.: Center for Strategic and International Studies, July 2006), xv. To be sure, the response of the reserve components has been exemplary, but constant employment of these troops and units is not what they were designed for—nor what reservists signed up for.

34. For a more thorough discussion of Army equipment needs, see Lawrence J. Korb, Loren B. Thompson, and Carolyn P. Wadhams, *Army Equipment after Iraq* (Washington, D.C.: Center for American Progress, 2006). The Army's National Guard has also been substantially affected in this regard: "More than 64,000 pieces of equipment have been left behind in Iraq, contributing to a $24 billion equipment shortfall as Guard units have only an estimated one-third of their essential gear on hand, according to the Government Accountability Office"; Ann Scott Tyson, "Possible Iraq Deployments Would Stretch Reserve Force," *Washington Post*, November 5, 2005, A1. See also Gary J. Schmitt, "Of Men and Materiel: The Crisis in Defense Spending," *National Security Outlook*, American Enterprise Institute, November 2006, http://www.aei.org/docLib/20061103_200611NSOg.pdf (accessed December 1, 2006).

35. U.S. Department of Defense, *Quadrennial Defense Review Report*, February 6, 2006, 9, http://www.defenselink.mil/pubs/pdfs/QDR20060203.pdf (accessed October 30, 2006).

36. Ibid., 10

37. George W. Bush, "President Addresses Nation, Discusses Iraq, War on Terror" (speech, Washington, D.C., The White House, June 28, 2005), http://www.whitehouse.gov/news/releases/2005/06/20050628-7.html (accessed November 14, 2006).

38. Theodore Roosevelt, "Washington's Forgotten Maxim" (address to the U.S. Naval War College, June 2, 1897), in Mario di Nunzio, ed., *Theodore Roosevelt: An American Mind* (New York: Penguin Books, 1994), 176.

39. Even before the wars in Afghanistan and Iraq, the U.S. military was extremely busy. As the House Armed Services Committee noted in the report accompanying the Defense Authorization Act for fiscal year 2001, "The U.S. armed forces were employed overseas more times in the past decade than in the previous 45 years. Since 1989, the Army has participated

in 35 major deployments"; House Committee on Armed Services, *Report on H.R. 4205, National Defense Authorization Act for Fiscal Year 2001*, report prepared by Floyd D. Spence, 106th Congress, 2d sess., May 12, 2000, 64-304, 1, http://armedservices.house.gov/billsandreports/106thcongress/hr4205 committeereport.pdf (accessed November 14, 2006).

40. Bradley Graham, "Pentagon Leaders Urge Accelerated 50% Boost in Procurement," *Washington Post*, November 11, 1995, A12.

41. In testimony before Congress prior to stepping down from his position as deputy secretary of defense, John Hamre noted that "even though [the Clinton administration] got to $60 billion in our modernization budget, we're still not really making up for the hole that we dug for ourselves during the 90s . . . actually the second half of the 80s and the 90s"; U.S. House of Representatives, Committee on Armed Services, *Report on H.R. 4205*, 15.

42. See Cordesman, "Trends in U.S. Defense Spending," 7. For an even direr estimate of the procurement budget problems, see Daniel Goure and Jeffrey M. Ranney, *Averting the Defense Train Wreck in the New Millennium* (Washington, D.C.: Center for Strategic and International Studies, 1999).

43. Congressional Budget Office, *Budgeting for Defense: Maintaining Today's Forces*, September 2000, summary, http://www.cbo.gov/showdoc. cfm?index=2398&sequence=1 (accessed October 30, 2006).

44. Ann Scott Tyson, "General says Army will need to grow," *Washington Post*, December 15, 2006, A1.

45. As cited in Dave Ahearn, "Weapons Systems Seem Unaffordable in Coming Years," *Defense Today*, February 22, 2006, 2.

46. See Congressional Budget Office, *The Long-Term Implications of Current Defense Plans and Alternatives: Summary Update for Fiscal Year 2006*, October 2005, http://www.cbo.gov/ftpdocs/67xx/doc6786/10-17-LT_Defense.pdf (accessed October 30, 2006), and Congressional Budget Office, *The Long-Term Implications of Current Defense Plans and Alternatives: Detailed Update for Fiscal Year 2006*, January 2006, http://www.cbo.gov/ftpdocs/70xx/doc7004/01-06-DPRDetailedUpdate.pdf (accessed October 30, 2006). See also Dave Ahearn, "Procurement Crunch Won't Be Averted by Ending Tax Cuts," *Defense Today*, February 2, 2006, 1; Richard Mullen, "Analysts See Gaps between Budget, QDR," *Defense Today*, February 10, 2006, 1; and Dave Ahearn, "Weapons Systems Seem Unaffordable in Coming Years," *Defense Today*, February 22, 2006, 1.

47. Lawrence B. Lindsey, "Guns and Butter: Promoting Economic Growth and Prosperity" (speech, Washington, D.C., Heritage Foundation, April 21, 2006), http://www.heritage.org/Press/Events/ev042106a.cfm (accessed October 30, 2006).

Chapter 2: Protracted Wars and the Army's Future

1. William A. Stofft and Charles E. Heller, *America's First Battles* (Lawrence, Kans.: University Press of Kansas, 1986).

2. John J. Garstka and Arthur K. Cebrowski, "Network-Centric Warfare: Its Origins and Future," *U.S. Naval Institute Proceedings* 124, no. 1 (January 1998): 28–35; John J. Garstka, David S. Alberts, and Frederick P. Stein, *Network Centric Warfare: Developing and Leveraging Information Superiority*, 2d ed. (Washington, D.C.: CCRP Publication Services, 1999); Harlan Ullman and James P. Wade, *Shock and Awe: Achieving Rapid Dominance* (Washington, D.C.: National Defense University Press, 1996); and Frederick W. Kagan, *Finding the Target: The Transformation of American Military Policy* (New York: Encounter Books, 2006) for an overview of the development of network-centric warfare and its ancillary concepts in the 1990s.

3. The 2006 Quadrennial Defense Review, for example, implicitly posits a rapid American withdrawal from both Iraq and Afghanistan; U.S. Department of Defense, *Quadrennial Defense Review Report*, February 6, 2006, http://www.defenselink.mil/pubs/pdfs/QDR20060203.pdf (accessed October 30, 2006).

4. See Gartzka and Cebrowski, "Network-Centric Warfare"; Gartzka, Alberts, and Stein, *Network Centric Warfare*; Kagan, *Finding the Target*; and U.S. Department of Defense, *Quadrennial Defense Review Report*, 2006.

5. John G. McGinn, James Dobbins, Keith Crane, Seth G. Jones, Rollie Lal, Andrew Rathmell, Rachel Swanger, and Anga Timilsina, *America's Role in Nation-Building from Germany to Iraq* (Arlington, Va.: RAND, 2003), 4–30. See also Frederick W. Kagan, "A Plan for Victory in Iraq: Defeat the Insurgents Militarily—Here's How," *Weekly Standard*, May 22, 2006, for a comparison of other force-ratio metrics of interest in the Iraq War. In general, it is clear that the more a postwar situation is allowed to deteriorate into insurgency, the higher the force ratios required to combat it, whereas adequate numbers of troops inserted immediately in the aftermath of combat reduce the likelihood of such a deterioration.

6. See Kagan, *Finding the Target*, and Frederick W. Kagan and Donald Kagan, *While America Sleeps: Self-Delusion, Military Weakness, and the Threat to Peace Today* (New York: St. Martin's Press, 2000) for a review of American defense policies in the 1990s.

7. See Frederick W. Kagan, "The Military's Manpower Crisis," *Foreign Affairs* 85, no. 4 (July–August 2006): 97–110, and Kagan, *Finding the Target*, to see these arguments in greater detail.

8. See Frederick W. Kagan, "Did We Fail in Afghanistan?" *Commentary* 115, no. 3 (March 2003): 39–45; Stephen Biddle, "Afghanistan and the Future of Warfare: Implications for Army and Defense Policy" (Carlisle, Pa.: U.S. Army War College, Strategic Studies Institute, 2002); and Kagan, *Finding the Target,* for examinations of the problems the U.S. approach to the Afghan conflict presented and the difficulties in applying that approach to other scenarios.

9. Colonel Fred Kienle, "The Need for Advisors: Generating an Iraqi Army from Scratch and Lessons for the Future" (working paper, American Enterprise Institute, Land Power Project, 2006).

10. Dobbins et al., *America's Role in Nation-Building,* argues cogently just how time-sensitive postwar deployments are in this regard.

11. Figuring the average cost of a brigade set of equipment at $1.5 billion (estimate based on widely varying costs of fielding M1/Bradley, Stryker, light infantry, and FCS-equipped brigades); the average annual personnel cost at $112,000 per service member; U.S. Government Accountability Office, "Military Personnel: DOD Needs to Improve the Transparency and Reassess the Reasonableness, Appropriateness, Affordability, and Sustainability of Its Military Compensation System," in *Report to Congressional Committees* (Washington, D.C.: Government Printing Office, 2005) and roughly doubling the current O&M budget of the force, since this proposal would nearly double the current complement of brigade combat teams.

12. Lawrence J. Korb, Loren B. Thompson, and Caroline P. Wadhams, *Army Equipment After Iraq* (Washington, D.C.: Center for American Progress and the Lexington Institute, 2006); and David S. C. Chu and Peter J. Shoomaker (Army general), "Resetting the Force: The Equipment Challenge," in *Torchbearer National Security Report* (Washington, D.C.: AUSA, 2006), 4–16.

13. And a great deal of solid work has been done along these lines by the CSIS Working Group on the National Guard and Reserves, part of the Beyond Goldwater-Nichols Project; Center for Strategic and International Studies, *The Future of the National Guard and Reserves: The Beyond Goldwater-Nichols Phase III Report,* July 2006, http://www.csis.org/media/csis/pubs/bgn_ph3_report.pdf (accessed November 21, 2006).

14. Some argue that homeland defense is or should be the National Guard's primary mission. It is clear that, for the foreseeable future at any event, the Guard will have to perform both roles.

Chapter 3: Age and Indifference Erode U.S. Air Power

1. Characterizations of official sentiments and actions in this essay are based in large part on discussions with senior government leaders inside and outside the Air Force. These exchanges have included two secretaries of the Air Force, two under secretaries, three chiefs of staff, two vice chiefs, and numerous other general officers.

2. Bruce Rolfsen, "On Lockdown: As Fleet Ages, U.S. Air Force Keeps One-Third of Planes Under Restrictions," *Defense News*, April 18, 2005; Loren Thompson, "Can the Space Sector Meet Military Goals for Space?" Lexington Institute, white paper, 2005, http://lexingtoninstitute.org/docs/662.pdf (accessed October 30, 2006).

3. Hampton Stevens, "USAF: Indian Exercises Showed Need For F/A-22, Changes in Training," *Inside the Air Force*, June 4, 2004, 1.

4. The officer who experienced this unusual failure was Lieutenant General David Deptula, then commander of Operation Northern Watch and now deputy chief of staff of the Air Force for intelligence.

5. Former Secretary of Defense William Cohen forcefully described the differences—and division of labor—between the F-22 and F-35 in a letter to Congressman Jerry Lewis on July 15, 1999. Cohen stated that "the F-22 will enable the Joint Strike Fighter to carry out its primary strike mission. The JSF was not designed for the air superiority mission, and redesigning it to do so will dramatically increase the cost."

6. These priorities were first described by presidential candidate George W. Bush in a speech entitled "A Period of Consequences" that was delivered at the Citadel in South Carolina on September 23, 1999. All of the Pentagon's subsequent pronouncements on military transformation once Bush was elected, such as the Defense Department's 2003 Transformation Planning Guidance, hewed closely to the original vision.

7. Glenn W. Goodman Jr., "Battle Manager in the Sky," *Intelligence, Surveillance & Reconnaissance Journal* (November–December 2003): 14–18.

8. Amy Butler, "Sunset for Airlifters?" *Aviation Week & Space Technology*, October 31, 2005.

9. Loren Thompson, "QDR Climax: Friendly Fire Hits the Joint Strike Fighter," Lexington Institute, issue brief, November 18, 2005, http://lexingtoninstitute.org/716.shtml (accessed October 30, 2006).

10. U.S. Department of Defense, *Quadrennial Defense Review Report*, 2006.

11. See U.S. Department of Defense, "Report of the Commission to Assess United States National Security Space Management and Organization,"

January 11, 2001, http://www.defenselink.mil/pubs/space20010111.html (accessed October 30, 2006).

12. See Thompson, *Can the Space Sector Meet Military Goals For Space?* 9–12.

13. U.S. Department of Defense, *Report of the Defense Science Board/Air Force Scientific Advisory Board Joint Task Force on Acquisition of National Security Space Programs* (Washington, D.C.: Government Printing Office, 2003), 1–4.

14. The most comprehensive exposition of future Air Force operational requirements can be found in the service's *U.S. Air Force Transformation Flight Plan*, released by the Department of the Air Force in 2004.

15. Concern about the need to establish and maintain information dominance permeates the *Quadrennial Defense Review Report*, particularly in the section entitled "Reorienting Capabilities and Forces," beginning on page 41; U.S. Department of Defense, *Quadrennial Defense Review Report*, 2006. The journalist who has most thoroughly covered what information dominance means for the Air Force is David Fulghum of *Aviation Week & Space Technology*. See, for example, his "Wireless War," in the October 24, 2005, issue of the magazine.

16. The most useful public resource for finding detailed description of all these programs is GlobalSecurity.org, at www.globalsecurity.org.

17. Greg Grant, "U.S. Army Drops C-130 Requirement for FCS," *Defense News*, September 26, 2005; Rebecca Christie, "Air Force Plan Spends $9B On Tankers In FY 2007–2001," *Dow Jones Newswires*, February 9, 2005.

18. In addition to the perilous financial state of many domestic carriers, there is a gradual shift underway from wide-body to narrow-body jets as the industry abandons "hub and spoke" route arrangements in favor of point-to-point plans. Narrow-body jets are less useful in military cargo missions.

19. See, for example, David Fulghum, "USAF Acknowledges Beam Weapon Readiness," *Aviation Week & Space Technology*, October 7, 2002, and David Fulghum, "Raptor Unwrapped," *Aviation Week & Space Technology*, May 24, 2004.

20. U.S. Department of Defense, *Report of the Commission to Assess United States National Security Space Management and Organization*, 12–15.

21. See the Rivet Joint program description at www.globalsecurity.org.

22. Christine Anderson, *Military Satellite Communications: Past, Present, Future* (Los Angeles, Calif.: MILSATCOM Joint Program Office, 2003), 17–30; Jeremy Singer, "USAF Emphasizing Risk Reduction in T-SAT Budgeting," *Space News*, February 21, 2005; Rebecca Christie, "DoD Shrinks

Radio Project To Trim Risk, Build Support," *Dow Jones Newswires*, May 3, 2006.

23. See the RQ-1 Predator and RQ-4 Global Hawk program descriptions at www.globalsecurity.org.

24. Loren Thompson, "After Many Mistakes, Military Space Is Coming Back," Lexington Institute, issue brief, May 24, 2006, http://lexingtoninstitute.org/788.shtml (accessed October 30, 2006); Warren Ferster, "USAF Buoyed by Progress on SBIRS," *Defense News*, October 9, 2006, 78; Glenn W. Goodman, "Space-Based Radar Heads to Next Stage," *Space News*, July 19, 2004.

25. Loren Thompson, "Lift," Lexington Institute, issue brief, April 13, 2006, http://lexingtoninstitute.org/788.shtml (accessed October 30, 2006).

26. "U.S. Debating Aerial Tanker Types, Mix," *Defense Industry Daily*, March 21, 2006.

27. Andrea Shalal-Esa, "U.S. Military Said Moving Ahead on New Bomber," Reuters Newswire, June 13, 2006.

28. William B. Scott, "Next-Gen Strike," *Aviation Week & Space Technology*, June 12, 2006.

29. Robert Wall and Craig Covault, "Eroding GPS Worries Pentagon," *Aviation Week & Space Technology*, November 4, 2002.

30. U.S. Air Force, *Air Force Recapitalization* (Washington, D.C.: Government Printing Office, 2006), 4.

31. U.S. Air Force, *FY2007 Unfunded Priority List*, http://wwwd.house .gov/hasc_democrats/Issues%20109th/unfunded/AF%20UFR%20FY07.pdf (accessed October 30, 2006).

32. See budget tables in the "2006 USAF Almanac" edition of *Air Force Magazine*, May 2006, 57–58.

Chapter 4: Numbers and Capabilities

1. Wayne P. Hughes Jr. (captain, USN, ret.), *Fleet Tactics and Coastal Combat*, 2d ed. (Annapolis, Md.: Naval Institute Press, 2000), 8–9.

2. Naval Historical Center, "U.S. Navy Active Ship Force Levels," Department of the Navy, http://www.history.navy.mil/branches/org9-4c.htm.

3. The call for a Navy that was the "greatest in the world" came from none other than Woodrow Wilson, during his run for president in 1916. At the time, he was chided by many for being so bold as to challenge the primacy of the British Royal Navy. See Kenneth J. Hagan, *This People's Navy* (New York: Free Press, 1991), 252.

4. Naval Historical Center, "U.S. Navy Active Ship Force Levels." A great recount of the trying years for the Battle Force after World War II is found in Hagan, "In Search of a Mission," *This People's Navy*, chapter 12.

5. Naval Historical Center, "U.S. Navy Active Ship Force Levels."

6. Ibid.

7. Beginning in 1917 and through the 1950s, the Soviet Navy was a minor regional navy. Transformed into a formidable force under the 1956–85 leadership of Admiral Sergey Gorshkov, it was about the same size as the U.S. Navy in terms of numbers of ships during the Cuban Missile Crisis in 1962, but qualitatively inferior in almost every category. By the 1970s, principally in two major "Okean" exercises, the Soviet Navy demonstrated its growing global power and its ability to contest the U.S. Navy in all oceans. For a short history of the Soviet Navy, see "Soviet Navy," http://en.wikipedia.org/wiki/Soviet_Navy (accessed November 15, 2006).

8. See James D. Watkins (admiral, USN), "The Maritime Strategy," supplement in *Proceedings* 112, no. 1 (January 1986): 2–17. For a more thorough discussion of its development, see Norman Freidman, *U.S. Maritime Strategy* (Annapolis, Md.: U.S. Naval Institute Press, 1988).

9. See John F. Lehman, "The 600-Ship Navy," supplement in *Proceedings* 112, no.1 (January 1986): 30–40.

10. The QDR did not explicitly designate a total ship battle force target of 302 ships; it described the fleet only in general terms. As a result, the 1997 QDR fleet is variously described as having between 300 and 310 ships. Based on notes and interviews, I have settled on 302 ships as being the actual 1997 QDR fleet target. See U.S. Department of Defense, *Report of the Quadrennial Defense Review*, May 1997, http://www.defenselink.mil/pubs/qdr (accessed October 30, 2006).

11. The only substantial difference between the 2001 QDR fleet and the 1997 QDR fleet was that its attack-submarine target was increased by five boats, from 50 to 55 SSNs.

12. Mike Mullen (vice admiral, USN), "Global Concept of Operations," *Proceedings* 129, no. 2 (April 2003): 66–69, http://www.usni.org/proceedings/Articles03/PROmullen04.htm (accessed November 15, 2006).

13. See Globalsecurity.org, "DD-963 Spruance-Class," http://www.globalsecurity.org/military/systems/ship/dd-963.htm (accessed November 15, 2006).

14. This was the number of ships listed in the *Naval Vessel Register* (NVR) on December 31, 2004. The NVR can be found online at http://www.nvr.navy.mil.

15. See for example Arthur Herman, "Our Incredible Shrinking Navy," *New York Post Online Edition*, June 9, 2005 (accessed June 10, 2005).

16. The Mk41 VLS, consisting of modules of missile storage and firing cells nestled into the hull of a ship, was more reliable, better protected, and offered higher rates of fire than previous missile launch systems. More importantly, they were much more space-efficient. On an identical hull, a VLS-equipped ship could carry 128 missiles, a non–VLS-equipped ship only 88. Moreover, the cells themselves can accommodate surface-to-air missiles, antisubmarine rockets, or land-attack missiles, allowing a warship's magazine load to be tailored flexibly to account for the most likely threat. For these reasons, every large surface combatant commissioned by the Navy since 1986 has been equipped with the VLS. See FAS Military Analysis Network, "Mk 41 Vertical Launch System," Federation of American Scientists, http://www.fas.org/man/dod-101/sys/ship/weaps/mk-41-vls.htm (accessed October 30, 2006).

17. See Robert O. Work (colonel, USMC, ret.), *The Challenge of Maritime Transformation: Is Bigger Better?* (Washington, D.C.: Center for Strategic and Budgetary Assessments, 2002), 70.

18. The calculations are as follows. 1989: 13 carriers x 162 aimpoints a day = 2,106 aimpoints a day; 2004: 11 carriers x 693 aimpoints a day = 7,623 aimpoints a day. Again, it is important to emphasize that these are simply theoretical maximums used for comparative purposes only. The number of aimpoints hit per day in a real-world operation, over long ranges, or in the face of credible air defense, would be much less. For a more sober view on the number of aimpoints that can be hit per day, see B. W. Stone (lieutenant, USN), "A Bridge Too Far," *Proceedings* 131, no. 2 (February 2005): 31–35.

19. See, for example, A. D. Baker III, "World Navies Are in Decline," *Proceedings* 130, no. 3 (March 2004): 32–49.

20. See Stephen Saunders (commodore, RN), ed., *Jane's Fighting Ships, 2004–2005*, 107th ed. (Surrey, England: Jane's Information Group, Ltd, 2004); and Eric Wertheim, ed., *Combat Fleets of the World 2005–2006* (Annapolis, Md.: U.S. Naval Institute Press, 2005).

21. Saunders, *Jane's Fighting Ships*; Wertheim, *Combat Fleets of the World*.

22. Department of the Navy, *Interim Report to Congress on Annual Long-Range Plan(s) for the Construction of Naval Vessels for FY 2006* (Washington, D.C.: Government Printing Office, March, 2005). For good summaries of this report, see Christopher P. Cavas, "U.S. Navy Sets 30-year Plan," *Defense News*, March 28, 2006; and David Ahearn, "Navy Carrier Force Drops to 10 in 2014, But Surge Ability Unchanged," *Defense Today*, April 5, 2005.

23. For a description of the Navy's complete plan, see U.S. Department of the Navy, *Report to Congress on the Long-Range Plan for Construction of*

Naval Vessels for FY 2007 (Washington, D.C.: Government Printing Office, 2006).

24. I am indebted to Dr. Eric Labs, Congressional Budget Office, for providing me with these figures.

25. Congressional Budget Office, *Options for the Navy's Future Fleet* (Washington, D.C.: Government Printing Office, May 2006), xvi.

26. These assumptions were illuminated by a series of briefings and discussions among Navy officials, the author, Ron O'Rourke, senior defense analyst at the Congressional Research Service, and Eric Labs from CBO's National Security Division.

27. Admiral Clark called for a diversion of funds from R&D to ship procurement, pointing out that the R&D budget in his last year was nearly $9 billion higher than when he took office in 2000; see Christopher P. Cavas, "U.S. CNO: Find Ship Funds in R&D," *Defense News*, July 11, 2005, 24.

28. Copy of the Navy's *FY 2007 Unfunded Deficiency List*, provided to the author by Steve Kosiak, senior budget analyst, CSBA.

29. See Office of the Secretary of Defense, Office of Force Transformation, *Alternative Fleet Architecture Design* (Washington, D.C.: Government Printing Office, 2005).

30. U.S. Department of Defense, *Quadrennial Defense Review Report*, February 6, 2006, http://www.defenselink.mil/pubs/pdfs/QDR20060203.pdf (accessed October 30, 2006).

31. For a good summary of the development of the AirLand Battle Doctrine, see John L. Romjue, "The Evolution of AirLand Battle Concept," *Air University Review* (May–June 1984), http://www.airpower.maxwell.af.mil/airchronicles/aureview/1984/may-jun/may-jun84.html (accessed October 19, 2006).

32. The references to Navy shipbuilding plans in the following sections come from two main sources: the aforementioned U.S. Department of the Navy, *Report to Congress on the Long-Range Plan for Construction of Naval Vessels for FY 2007*; and J. F. McCarthy Jr. (captain, USN), "Recapitalizing the Navy's Battle Line," a PowerPoint presentation given at a Department of the Navy Media Roundtable on June 8, 2006.

33. The French, Brazilian, and Russian navies operate one each.

34. This plan assumes Congress will approve the early retirement of the conventionally powered *John F. Kennedy*.

35. David Brown, "Ready to Hone Ship's Details," *Defense News*, April 12, 2004; Christopher P. Cavas, "DoD Cancels Review of Healthy CVN-21 Program," *Defense News*, June 6, 2005; and Lorenzo Cortes. "CVN-21

Will Be the 'Big Hammer' of ESF, Admiral Says," *Defense Daily*, April 9, 2004, 4.

36. Lorenzo Cortes, "Navy Aims For Higher CVN-21 Sortie Rate Over Current *Nimitz*-class Aircraft Carriers," *Defense News*, January 23, 2004; and Geoff Fein, "Navy Wants Reduced Crew Size, Lower Costs for CVN-21," *Defense Daily*, June 3, 2005.

37. Congressional Budget Office, *Options for the Navy's Future Fleet*, 15, 19.

38. John Shank et al., *Modernizing the U.S. Aircraft Carrier Fleet: Accelerating CVN-21Production Versus Mid-Life Modernization* (Santa Monica, Calif.: RAND Corporation, 2005), xiii–xvii.

39. Ronald O'Rourke, "Navy-Marine Corps Amphibious and Maritime Prepositioning Ship Programs: Background and Oversight Issues for Congress," CRS-8, March 29, 2005, http://www.globalsecurity.org/military/library/report/crs/crs_rl32513.pdf (accessed October 31, 2006).

40. In accordance with the idea of SeaAir Littoral Battle, the "J" in the CVE designator reflects the fact that Air Force STOVL JSFs could also operate off these ships, if that service purchases these aircraft as now planned.

41. Norman Polmar, "Submarines Under Attack," *Proceedings* 131, no. 6 (June 2005): 89.

42. The first four SSGNs were former SSBNs designed to carry and fire the C-4 version of the Trident submarine-launched ballistic missile (SLBM). All remaining SSBNs carry the larger D5 missile, which would require additional engineering work to convert. From interviews with officials from Electric Boat concerning the submarine design base.

43. For example, a ten-boat SSBN force carrying a total of 240 Trident D5 missiles (24 missiles per boat) with seven reentry vehicles per warhead (the D-5 can carry up to eight) can carry up 1,680 "countable" warheads—close to the maximum NPR target of 1,750 submarine warheads. Norman Polmar, *Ships and Aircraft of the U.S. Fleet*, 18th ed. (Annapolis, Md.: Naval Institute Press, 2005), 68–79.

44. Richard Fisher Jr., "Growing Asymmetries in the China-Japan Naval Balance," International Assessment and Strategy Center, November 22, 2005, http://www.strategycenter.net/research/pubID.83/pub_detail.asp (accessed November 30, 2005).

45. Ibid.

46. Russian fleet numbers are taken from Globalsecurity.org, "Russian Warships," http://www.globalsecurity.org/military/world/russia/ship.htm (accessed November 15, 2006). U.S. numbers are taken from Naval Historical Center, "Ship Force Levels, 1886–Present," http://www.history.navy.mil/branches/org9-4c.htm (accessed October 30, 2006).

47. For a discussion of how the U.S. Navy is approaching UUVs, see Robert A. Hamilton, "The Brain-Based Controller: A New Concept for Underwater Vehicles," *Seapower* 48, no.7 (July 2005): 26–29.

48. Small combatants are defined here as vessels with full load displacements below 3,000 tons. For a discussion about small combatants in the U.S. Navy, see Robert O. Work, *Naval Transformation and the Littoral Combat Ship* (Washington, D.C.: Center for Strategic and Budgetary Assessments, 2004).

49. See Globalsecurity.org, "Littoral Combat Ship (LCS)," http://www.globalsecurity.org/military/systems/ship/lcs.htm (accessed November 15, 2006), and Work, *Naval Transformation and the Littoral Combat Ship*.

50. See, for example, McCarthy Jr., "Recapitalizing the Navy's Battle Line."

51. Admiral Mullen, chief of naval operations, unveiled the concept of global fleet stations at a speech at the Current Strategy Forum, Newport, R.I., on June 14, 2006.

52. I am indebted to Dr. Eric Labs, Congressional Budget Office, for explaining the Navy's crewing plans for the LCS.

53. The AEGIS remains "the most advanced anti-air warfare system in existence, land based or naval"; see Polmar, *Ships and Aircraft of the U.S. Fleet*, 135.

54. The original target was for $750 million in FY 1998 dollars; see Global Security, "DD-21 Zumwalt," http://www.globalsecurity.org/military/systems/ship/dd-21.htm (accessed November 15, 2006).

55. This information was provided by the Navy to Dr. Eric Labs, national security specialist at the Congressional Budget Office. Dr. Labs conveyed this information to the author in August 2006.

56. C. H. Goddard (captain, USN) and C. B. Marks (commander, USN), "DD(X) Navigates Uncharted Waters," *Proceedings* 131, no. 1 (January 2005): 31.

57. Another argument for making the DDG-1000 a technology demonstrator is that the preferred solution for its integrated power system, the permanent magnet motor (PMM), will not be ready for the class. U.S. submariners are hoping that a PMM will someday power future U.S. submarines. A single AIM DDG-1000 technology demonstrator would allow the battle fleet to test thoroughly all aspects of a new, all-electric-drive surface combatant as it waits for the maturation of the PMM. A common electric motor for the aforementioned USW as well as future surface combatants would result in significant O&M and training savings for the future fleet. Rati Bishnoi, "Lawmaker Wants DD(X) 'Magnet Motor,'" Military.com, April 14, 2006, http://www.military.com/features/0,15240,94163,00.html (accessed October 30, 2006).

58. For more details, as well as a brief history of the amphibious-lift requirement, see Matthew T. Robinson, *Integrated Amphibious Operations Update Study (DoN Lift 2+): A Short History of the Amphibious Lift Requirement* (Alexandria, Va.: Center for Naval Analyses, July 2002).

59. The "10-30-30" metric was developed during Operational Availability 2003, a joint staff planning effort that took place after the overthrow of the Taliban in Afghanistan but before Operation Iraqi Freedom. The study came in response to queries from the secretary of defense on the planning metrics being used for simultaneous or overlapping major regional contingencies. This audacious goal was the logical combination of a defense strategy that required the U.S. armed forces to be able to win two "overlapping" or near-simultaneous major combat operations against traditional conventional opponents, and an increasing U.S. emphasis on "rapid decisive operations" since the end of the Cold War. See Greg Jaffe, "Battle Lines: Rumsfeld's Push for Speed Fuels Pentagon Dissent," *Wall Street Journal*, May 16, 2005; and Globalsecurity.org, "Rapid Decisive Operations," http://www.globalsecurity.org/military/ops/rdo.htm (accessed November 15, 2006).

60. Squadron costs are also found in "Maritime Prepositioning Force (Future) Shipbuilding Requirements," a PowerPoint presentation to Hill staffers by the Marine Corps Combat Development Center, June 2005.

61. Center for Naval Analyses, *U.S. Naval Responses to Situations, 1970–1999* (Alexandria, Va.: Center for Strategic Studies, 2000).

62. Again, the best study of U.S. postwar amphibious lift requirements is found in Robinson, *Integrated Amphibious Operations*.

Chapter 5: The Marine Corps

1. U.S. Department of Defense, *Quadrennial Defense Review Report*, February 6, 2006, http://www.defenselink.mil/pubs/pdfs/QDR20060203. pdf (accessed October 30, 2006)

2. Mike Hagee (general, USMC), "Creating Stability in an Unstable World," *Marine Corps Gazette*, July 2005.

3. For implications and further details for all of the U.S. armed forces, as well as other homeland security agencies, see F. G. Hoffman, "Complex Irregular War: The Next Revolution in Military Affairs," *Orbis* 50, no. 3 (Summer 2006): 395–411.

4. U.S. Department of Defense, *Quadrennial Defense Review Report*, 2006, 35–37.

5. Ibid., 36.

6. Ibid., 11.

7. These phrases are clearly drawn from Basil Liddell Hart, "The Indirect Approach," in *Strategy*, rev. ed., (New York: Macmillan, 1967), 327–29.

8. U.S. Marine Corps, *Concepts and Programs*, by M. W. Hagee (Washington, D.C.: Government Printing Office, 2005), 25–33.

9. Fred Kagan, "A Strategy for Heroes," *Weekly Standard*, February 20, 2006.

10. U.S. Department of Defense, *Quadrennial Defense Review Report*, 2006, 18.

11. Ibid., 27–29.

12. For key excerpts of this unsigned policy guidance, see PNAC.info, "1992 'Defense Planning Guidance' Draft Excerpts," April 25, 2003, http://pnac.info/index.php/2003/1992-defense-planning-guidance-draft-excerpts/ (accessed November 9, 2006).

13. M. Elaine Bunn, "Force Posture and Dissuasion," *Strategic Insight* 3, no. 10 (October 2004), http://www.ccc.nps.navy.mil/si/2004/oct/bunnOct04 .asp (accessed December 1, 2006).

14. The report itself, however, is generally silent on what it will take to recruit, train, and retain an adequately sized force in the future. Only the need to attract and retain special skills for irregular warfare, including linguists and foreign area officers, is adequately covered. But the need to address other personnel issues, such as a junior officer and noncommissioned officer (NCO) corps exhausted by multiple combat tours, is left untouched. Without a concerted effort to retain the best combat-experienced young officers and NCOs, the future military will face a hollowed-out leadership cadre.

15. The QDR also avoids the realities of higher expenditures for wear and tear on equipment. While the force may be battle-hardened and highly experienced, material readiness cannot be ignored. The QDR never acknowledges the need to replace destroyed or worn-out equipment, and there is no mention of the significant resources required to reset the force. Supplemental funding has been helpful, but the armed forces will have large holes, especially in the readiness accounts that maintain their ammunition stocks, trucks, and other mobility assets, and in other materiel assets that are worn out by their use in Iraq and Afghanistan. This is what the services are referring to as their "reset" costs in their budget requests.

16. This debate aired at the American Enterprise Institute in a day-long program on the Marine Corps entitled, "The Future of the United States Marine Corps," Washington, D.C., August 18, 2005. A transcript of this event can be accessed at: http://www.aei.org/events/filter.all,eventID.1093/transcript.asp.

17. Max Boot, "The Corps Should Look to its Small Wars Past," *Armed Forces Journal International* (March 2006), http://www.armedforcesjournal.com/2006/03/1813950 (accessed December 1, 2006).

18. Ralph Peters, *New Glory, Expanding America's Global Supremacy* (New York: Sentinel, 2005), 327–37.

19. F. G. Hoffman, "Forcible Entry is a Strategic Necessity," *Proceedings* 130, no. 1 (November 2004): 5.

20. U.S. Department of Defense, *Quadrennial Defense Review Report*, 2006, 11.

21. According to U.S. Code Title 10 C, Chapter 507, Section 5063a, "The Marine Corps, within the Department of the Navy, shall be so organized as to include not less than three combat divisions and three air wings, and such other land combat, aviation, and other services as may be organic therein." But because the law does not define what a division or wing is, the Corps is able to fudge this requirement. For example, the Marine Corps cut out of its force structure in recent years an entire Marine regiment and several artillery battalions to meet imposed budget ceilings.

22. John G. Castelaw (lieutentant general, USMC), "The State of Marine Aviation," *Marine Corps Gazette*, May 2006, 13–18.

23. Max Boot, *The Savage Wars of Peace: Small Wars and the Rise of American Power* (New York: Perseus Books, 2002).

24. Max Boot, "The Corps Should Look to its Small Wars Past," 17–18.

25. U.S. Department of Defense, *Quadrennial Defense Review Report*, 2006, 36.

26. Michael J. Mazarr, "Extremism, Terror and the Future of Conflict," Policy Review Online, March 10, 2006, www.policyreview.org/000/mazarr.html (accessed October 30, 2006).

27. For more in-depth discussion on this point, see Stephen Biddle, "Afghanistan and the Future of Warfare," *Foreign Affairs* 82, no. 2 (March/April 2003): 31–46.

28. Brian Michel Jenkins, "Redefining the Enemy," *RAND Review* 28, no. 1 (Spring 2004): 17.

29. Thomas X. Hammes, *The Sling and Stone: On War in the 21st Century* (St. Paul, Minn.: Zenith, 2005), 1.

30. For a detailed summary of how this occurred, see John Simeoni (lieutenant colonel, Australian Army), "U.S. Marine Urban Combined-Arms Operations in Iraq: Some Observations," *Australian Army Journal* 2, no. 2 (Autumn 2005): 89–99.

31. Robert E. Schmidle and F. G. Hoffman, "Commanding the Contested Zone," *Proceedings* 130, no. 9 (September 2004): 49–54.

32. Ralph Peters, "Our Soldiers, Their Cities," *Parameters* 26, no. 1 (Spring 1996): 43–50.

33. National Intelligence Council, *Global Trends 2015: A Dialogue About the Future with Nongovernmental Experts* (Washington, D.C.: National Intelligence Council, 2000), 6, 15.

34. For a more detailed exploration see F. G. Hoffman, "Expeditionary Maneuver Brigades," in Sam Tangredi, ed., *Globalization and Maritime Forces* (Washington, D.C.: Institute for National Security Studies, National War College, 2003).

35. Gayle Putrich, "GAO: Marine Corps' EFV Program Tops $12 Billion," *Defense News*, May 1, 2006, 17; Renae Merle, "Marine Corps Amphibious Vehicle Cost Surges 45%," *Washington Post*, May 3, 2006, D3.

36. Michael S. Groen, "Blue Diamond Intelligence, Division Level Intelligence Operations During OIF," *Marine Corps Gazette*, February 2004, 22–25.

37. Max Boot, among others, has suggested an existing S-92 model, or the naval version of the SH-60 Blackhawk; Max Boot, "The Corps Should Look to Its Small Wars Past."

38. U.S. Department of Defense, *Quadrennial Defense Review Report*, 2006, 36.

39. In his latest book, strategist Colin Gray characterizes future conflict as a blurring of regular and irregular warfare; Colin S. Gray, *Another Bloody Century: Future Warfare* (London: Weidenfeld & Nicolson, 2006), 212.

40. James N. Mattis and F. G. Hoffman, "The Rise of Hybrid Wars," *Proceedings* 131, no. 11 (November 2005): 18–19.

41. F. G. Hoffman, "How Marines are Preparing for Hybrid Wars," *Armed Forces Journal International* (March 2006), http://www.armedforcesjournal.com/2006/03/1813952/ (accessed December 1, 2006).

42. General M. W. Hagee, "Statement Before the Senate Armed Services Committee," March 9, 2006, 4–5, http://armed-services.senate.gov/statemnt/2006/March/Hagee%2003-09-06.pdf (accessed November 10, 2006).

43. Jason Sherman, "Marines Cut, Kill Programs To Improve Regular Warfare Capabilities," *Inside the Pentagon*, August 24, 2006, 1.

44. Lawrence J. Korb, Max A. Bergmann, and Loren B. Thompson, *Marine Corps Equipment After Iraq* (Washington, D.C.: Center for American Progress, 2006), 3.

45. Victor David Hanson, *A War Like No Other: How the Athenians and Spartans Fought the Peloponnesian War* (New York: Random House, 2005), 235–69.

About the Authors

Thomas Donnelly is a resident fellow in defense and security policy studies at the American Enterprise Institute. He is the coauthor of AEI's *National Security Outlook*. He is also the author of *The Military We Need* (AEI Press, 2005). He has worked previously as policy group director and a professional staff member for the Committee on National Security (now the Committee on Armed Services) in the U.S. House of Representatives. He is a former editor of *Armed Forces Journal*, *Army Times* and *Defense News*.

Francis G. Hoffman is a research fellow at the U.S. Marine Corps Center for Emerging Threats and Opportunities and an appointed member of the National Security Study Group with the U.S. Com-mission on National Security/21st Century. Mr. Hoffman is a former Marine Corps infantry officer and has served as director of the Strategic Studies Group for the Marine Corps Combat Development Command.

Frederick W. Kagan is a resident scholar at the American Enterprise Institute. He is a former associate professor at the United States Military Academy (West Point) and is an expert on the American military and defense issues. Mr. Kagan's most recent book is *Finding the Target: The Transformation of American Military Policy* (Encounter Books, 2006).

Gary J. Schmitt is a resident scholar at the American Enterprise Institute and director of AEI's program on advanced strategic studies, where he focuses on long-term strategic issues that will affect America's security at home and its ability to lead abroad. Mr. Schmitt is a former staff director of the Senate Select Committee on Intelligence and was executive director of the President's Foreign Intelligence Advisory Board (PFIAB).

Loren Thompson is the chief operating officer of the Lexington Institute, where he oversees the security studies program. He is an expert on military affairs, in particular the air force and military technology. He is currently an adjunct professor at Georgetown University. Mr. Thompson heads Source Associates, a consulting firm, and has written frequently on military affairs.

Robert O. Work is a senior analyst at the Center for Strategic and Budgetary Assessments. He is an expert on defense strategy, defense transformation, and maritime affairs, and is currently an adjunct professor at The George Washington University. Mr. Work served in the United States Marine Corps for twenty-seven years and has worked at the Office of Net Assessment, Office of the Secretary of Defense.

Research Staff

Gerard Alexander
Visiting Scholar

Joseph Antos
Wilson H. Taylor Scholar in Health
Care and Retirement Policy

Leon Aron
Resident Scholar

Claude E. Barfield
Resident Scholar; Director, Science
and Technology Policy Studies

Roger Bate
Resident Fellow

Walter Berns
Resident Scholar

Douglas J. Besharov
Joseph J. and Violet Jacobs
Scholar in Social Welfare Studies

Edward Blum
Visiting Fellow

Dan Blumenthal
Resident Fellow

Karlyn H. Bowman
Resident Fellow

John E. Calfee
Resident Scholar

Charles W. Calomiris
Visiting Scholar

Lynne V. Cheney
Senior Fellow

Steven J. Davis
Visiting Scholar

Mauro De Lorenzo
Resident Fellow

Veronique de Rugy
Research Fellow

Thomas Donnelly
Resident Fellow

Nicholas Eberstadt
Henry Wendt Scholar in Political
Economy

Mark Falcoff
Resident Scholar Emeritus

Gerald R. Ford
Distinguished Fellow

John C. Fortier
Research Fellow

Ted Frank
Resident Fellow; Director,
AEI Liability Project

David Frum
Resident Fellow

David Gelernter
National Fellow

Reuel Marc Gerecht
Resident Fellow

Newt Gingrich
Senior Fellow

James K. Glassman
Resident Fellow; Editor-in-Chief,
The American Magazine

Jack L. Goldsmith
Visiting Scholar

Robert A. Goldwin
Resident Scholar Emeritus

Kenneth P. Green
Resident Scholar

Michael S. Greve
John G. Searle Scholar

Robert W. Hahn
Resident Scholar; Director,
AEI-Brookings Joint Center
for Regulatory Studies

Kevin A. Hassett
Resident Scholar; Director,
Economic Policy Studies

Steven F. Hayward
F. K. Weyerhaeuser Fellow

Robert B. Helms
Resident Scholar; Director,
Health Policy Studies

Frederick M. Hess
Resident Scholar; Director,
Education Policy Studies

Ayaan Hirsi Ali
Resident Fellow

R. Glenn Hubbard
Visiting Scholar

Frederick W. Kagan
Resident Scholar

Leon R. Kass
Hertog Fellow

Herbert G. Klein
National Fellow

Marvin H. Kosters
Resident Scholar Emeritus

Irving Kristol
Senior Fellow Emeritus

Desmond Lachman
Resident Fellow

Michael A. Ledeen
Freedom Scholar

Adam Lerrick
Visiting Scholar

Phillip I. Levy
Resident Fellow

James R. Lilley
Senior Fellow

Lawrence B. Lindsey
Visiting Scholar

John H. Makin
Visiting Scholar

N. Gregory Mankiw
Visiting Scholar

Aparna Mathur
Research Fellow

Mark B. McClellan
Visiting Senior Fellow

Allan H. Meltzer
Visiting Scholar

Thomas P. Miller
Resident Fellow

Joshua Muravchik
Resident Scholar

Charles Murray
W. H. Brady Scholar

Roger F. Noriega
Visiting Fellow

Michael Novak
George Frederick Jewett Scholar
in Religion, Philosophy, and Public
Policy; Director, Social and Political
Studies

Norman J. Ornstein
Resident Scholar

Richard Perle
Resident Fellow

Alex J. Pollock
Resident Fellow

Sarath Rajapatirana
Visiting Fellow

Michael Rubin
Resident Scholar

Sally Satel
Resident Scholar

Gary Schmitt
Resident Scholar; Director,
AEI's Program on Advanced
Strategic Studies

Joel Schwartz
Visiting Fellow

Vance Serchuk
Research Fellow

Daniel Shaviro
Visiting Scholar

Kent Smetters
Visiting Scholar

Christina Hoff Sommers
Resident Scholar

Samuel Thernstrom
Managing Editor, AEI Press;
Director, W. H. Brady Program

Fred Thompson
Visiting Fellow

Richard Vedder
Visiting Scholar

Alan D. Viard
Resident Scholar

Mario Villarreal
Research Fellow

Peter J. Wallison
Resident Fellow

Ben J. Wattenberg
Senior Fellow

John Yoo
Visiting Scholar